Joan Wyndham

CW00346358

was brought up as a strict C̲...
religious companion, and was...
convent. After a period at RADA, ...
five years. Following the Second World War, she had a
series of jobs, ranging from running Oxford's first espresso
bar and cooking at the Royal Court Theatre to journalism
in Fleet Street. She is married, has two grown-up daughters
and lives in Chelsea.

Also by Joan Wyndham

LOVE LESSONS
LOVE IS BLUE

JOAN WYNDHAM

Anything Once

Flamingo
An Imprint of HarperCollinsPublishers

Flamingo
An Imprint of HarperCollins*Publishers*,
77–85 Fulham Palace Road,
Hammersmith, London W6 8JB

Published by Flamingo 1993
9 8 7 6 5 4 3 2 1

First published in Great Britain by
Sinclair-Stevenson Ltd 1992

Copyright © Joan Wyndham 1992

The Author asserts the moral right to
be identified as the author of this work

ISBN 0 00 654532 7

Printed in Great Britain by
HarperCollinsManufacturing, Glasgow

All rights reserved. No part of this publication may be
reproduced, stored in a retrieval system, or transmitted,
in any form or by any means, electronic, mechanical,
photocopying, recording or otherwise, without the prior
permission of the publishers.

This book is sold subject to the condition that it shall not,
by way of trade or otherwise, be lent, re-sold, hired out or
otherwise circulated without the publisher's prior consent
in any form of binding or cover other than that in which it
is published and without a similar condition including this
condition being imposed on the subsequent purchaser.

Chapter One

I was woken early by the cold November sunshine filtering through the dirty window panes of 32 Cadogan Street and felt immediately a sense of panic – the war was over and for the first time in five years I was in a room by myself, without the comforting sound of friends waking around me.

Frightening decisions lay ahead. What should I wear, now that the safe anonymity of a uniform had been taken from me? What to do with my day, jobless and faced by the awesome prospect of endless leave? I was beginning to realise that now I was no longer in the WAAF I would have to recreate my world from scratch every morning. All I had to my credit was a knowledge of radar, and the dubious ability to drill a squad of women on the parade ground – not much bloody use to me now.

My only possessions, apart from a dusty gramophone and a stack of Fats Waller records, were my portrait in charcoal by Petya, the young Czech artist I had once loved, – and my grandmother's sagging green divan on which she had once entertained Field Marshal Lord French when giving him the Lady Hamilton treatment in World War 1.

From downstairs came the reassuring whirr of my landlord, Mr Jaques the tailor, at his sewing-machine – apart from that, silence. I hadn't realised I was going to feel so lonely, with no one to laugh or gossip with, no focus to my life. I must have been mad to turn down Oxford for fear of losing my newly-won freedom for another form of discipline. Now, every evening, there would be that panicky search to find someone to go out with.

I lit the popping gas fire, and set about making myself look decent. After a brief wash in the freezing bathroom I took the pipe-cleaners out of my hair and combed it under into a page-boy, and put on some Max Factor Pancake No 2, some Coty powder, and a dash of Yardley's cherry lipstick. I thought about putting in my contact lenses but they were very painful, and after all there were no men around to see me, so I put on my glasses instead. Now I was ready to face the world.

The first problem, of course, was money. I had a £60 gratuity from the Air Force – about enough to pay the first nine months' rent – but I needed to double it fast. There was one useful skill I had picked up in the WAAF, and that was how to play the dogs. White City was on Saturday, and I rather fancied a dog called Northern Hero over the hurdles. Hurdle races are always the best, because there are fewer dogs involved, and I liked to do a lot of forecasts. On the other hand I didn't really want to break into my £60 while I still had a few things to sell, so I filled a suitcase with expensive ballet books – relics of my teenage balletomania – and set off for Foyle's. Out went Massine and Baronova, Lifar and Riabouchinska, and back came twelve lovely pound notes, enough for 120 two-bob tickets on the 7.30 at White City.

I put on a dirty old mac with the money secreted in an inside pocket and set off to make my fortune. Apart from the Hero there was only one other fancied dog, Kerry Dancer, but the odds would be bad on the two together, so I decided to use my Dad's old system called 'ekers and spreaders' – you eke out your money with a small covering bet on Hero and the Dancer, and spread like mad on a really crazy combination of favourites and outsiders.

The hare shot out, the dogs streaked after it, two favourites in the lead, but halfway through the first lap the Dancer lagged behind and my beautiful little outsider tucked her nose right under the Hero's tail. There's nothing in the world more exciting than watching your dogs come home in the right order, while you jump up and down and yell your head off. It was a £2 forecast so my fiver won me £200. 'Cor!' said the payout man, 'you'd better be careful with all that dosh!' So I put it in a little leather pouch and hung it round my neck under the mac and went off to buy some jellied eels. Then I went home to impress my Mum who nearly had a heart attack when I casually strewed my winnings out on her coffee table.

She and her companion Sid were still sharing the same tiny flat in Nell Gwynne House that they'd been in since their house was bombed. Sid had a camp bed in the bathroom.

My mother had lived with Sidonie ever since I could remember. My father, whom she had divorced when I was two, was only a ghost in the background, a shadowy, romantic figure whom I very rarely saw. Instead I read about him in glossy magazines – his paintings, his travel books, his house parties for smart intellectual friends, and his new job as Special Correspondent for the *Sunday Times*.

I need hardly say that my mother was not a lesbian. Converted to Catholicism soon after the divorce and living with a deeply religious lady, she hardly knew what lesbians were, let alone what they *did*! Mind you, she had a lot of rather odd lady friends, like Fiona who had to shave twice a day, and Bobby who spoke in a deep bass voice and bred bull-terriers.

I decided it was time I saw my father again, and plucked up enough courage to call him. He had a rather grand suite in the Hyde Park Hotel where he stayed between journalistic assignments for his newspaper. I'd heard he was just back from Cairo, where he'd been flipping around in his little aeroplane getting scoops ahead of his rivals.

When I came in he was busy scribbling away at his desk and all I could see was the brown sunburnt tonsure on the top of his head where he was going bald. He looked up, stared at me myopically, and finally recognised me as his daughter.

'Just a minute, Joanie, got to finish my swindle sheet for the *Sunday Times*!' I suppose he meant his expenses – mostly phoney – which seemed to cover several sheets of paper. He poured two enormous whiskies, and asked about my life. I told him how lonely and boring it was in London. For some reason this seemed to make him rather cross. 'Oh, reallah?' he said, in his ridiculously exaggerated upper-class accent. 'Now why is that, Joanie? I mean look at your cousin Annie Fleming, *she* seems to be having a jolly amusing time!' I had no idea who Annie Fleming was, but 'cousin' seemed to be a convenient sort of word for distant relatives who didn't want to know you. Anyway, my Dad now seemed to feel he must do something about my social life, and he told me he'd pick me up at seven o'clock for dinner at Cyril Connolly's.

I put on my best black dress and the velvet snood secured with kirbygrips and looked pretty good, if I say so myself. Daddy picked me up at seven, looking a bit horrified at the poverty of my lodgings, and we took a taxi to Somerset Place. It was a beautiful old house and filled with quite terrifyingly smart and intelligent people. Cyril himself was fat and piggy with one of those clever-ugly faces like Dylan Thomas had. His girlfriend Lys was like some exquisite little oriental concubine and wore a cheongsam.

At dinner I found myself next to a dark, handsome, foreign man with a deeply-lined face, who was introduced to me as Arthur Koestler.

Lys tripped in with a big dish of tiny birds called ortalans, which are almost impossible to eat except with your fingers. I thought that would be too rude, so speared one on my fork and it shot across the table and fell on the floor. Koestler retrieved it deftly.

'Don't worry,' he said, 'no one noticed. You're terrified, aren't you?' he went on, looking at me pityingly. 'But don't worry, my dear, your Uncle Arthur will look after you.' Apparently he and my Dad were both in love with the same girl, so he felt that made him a kind of relation.

More brilliant people arrived after dinner, like Stephen Spender and Peter Quennell, and everybody was being terribly bitchy about everybody else. It was like being in a nest of intellectual vipers. Nice Angela Thirkell was referred to as 'Arsenic and old lace', and everybody seemed to loathe poor Koestler, and called him a phoney communist. As for Connolly, he was known as 'Squirrel'. When he went out of the room a young man leapt onto a stool and did a wicked impersonation of him and everybody screamed 'Oh, darling, you've got Squirrel to a T!' I felt altogether embarrassed and out of my depth, so Daddy finally took me home. 'Most of my friends seemed to think you're rather prettah!' he told me in a voice of disbelief. This made me feel a lot more cheerful.

Zoe Hicks, my old friend from the WAAF days, Augustus John's daughter, moved into my flat for a few days. It was nice having company, but I wished she wouldn't borrow all my clothes when she went to parties. Half my best dresses seemed to have wine stains, or splits under the arms and hems put up with safety pins.

I had a wonderful day with Kit, on leave from Scotland – his demob hadn't come through yet. He still seemed very fond of me, and I thought him the nicest boy-friend I had ever had. He brought his guitar and a new Fats Waller record called 'Your Feets Too Big'. We played it again and again; then the actor Jon Pertwee came round, and they had a great guitar jam session together.

Before long I was making £2 a week working for my old ARP chum Ralph at Brechin Place. He made plastic goldfish and seaweed for ornamental tanks and I had to cut them out. Unfortunately he also made me hang them by my hairs for greater invisibility. Pulling them out was very painful and I felt I was in danger of going bald. My old flame Rupert from the Redcliffe Road days, who I still occasionally saw, told me he could get me a much better job running a hotel for some rather eccentric friends of his. It was called the Chartwell Hotel, and was run by an ex-silent movie star called Veronica and her young lover, whom she was seeing through college. They were going off to do a currency fiddle in Switzerland soon, and wanted someone to run the place while they were away. My helper at the hotel was called Robin. We were to charge £1 per night or £2 for a double, which was *outrageous*! We were both too embarrassed to ask for it, even to Americans, so we decided to lower the prices even though Veronica would be furious on her return.

It was very difficult to get any laundry done so we invented a technique of ironing the sheets on the bed. Sometimes we only just got the iron unplugged from the bedside lamp as the customer came thundering up the stairs, very surprised to find that his sheets were hot. Most of the customers were very polite and clean but there was one dreadful old satyr, a writer called Bernard Sudgen, whose personal habits were so revolting that we removed his sheets with fire tongs and brushed them down the stairs with a broom.

On my first day I turned up to do the breakfasts wearing my old WAAF uniform dyed a very smart forest green, pulled in tight with a leather belt, and my contact lenses. They were like goldfish bowls, and made my eyes look twice their size.

'Vous avez des yeux extraordinaires,' said a middle-aged Frenchman, as I handed him some burnt toast and a rather plastic-looking fishcake which Robin had salvaged from a previous customer's plate. These fish cakes were quite appalling – they had been dyed pink to look like salmon, and nobody ate them. Robin insisted that we reheat them for the next customer, though by this time they were so hard they gave out a ringing sound when you tapped them with your fork.

Apart from Robin my only other help was a slut called Sadie who pinched the customers' underwear and could usually be seen with six inches of fancy French lace hanging down below her filthy apron.

Rations were difficult. We depended almost entirely on an enormous Polish lady called the Princess Kadja who wore purple powder and reeked of cheap scent. Her brother was a Polish wholesale grocer, who got us everything we needed. The princess's English was a bit peculiar to say the least. 'Derleengs! Today I become for you a beautiful tin of frankfurters – the tin is a little – how do you say, blown? – but inside he ees all delicious.' At Christmas she promised to 'become' for us an enormous turkey.

I slept in a bunk bed in the attic and was blissfully happy. It was so wonderful to be working again and to be with people all the time. Alas, it didn't last. The week before Veronica and her lover were due back from fiddling money in Switzerland, a bailiff arrived at the door and said he'd come to take away all the furniture. We were powerless to stop him, and rather than stick around to face the undoubted wrath of V. and her boyfriend, who would certainly think it was all our fault, we decided to close the hotel and flee.

I was now back in my little room with only Kit's occasional visits to look forward to. I found myself falling more and more in love with him, and began to hope he might feel the same about me. Then one morning the blow fell. A letter arrived saying he'd fallen madly in love with a WAAF in Nottingham and was going to marry her. He thought it best if we never saw each other again. He admitted that he had never enjoyed sex so much as he had with me, but he felt I was some kind of witch who had him under her spell – in short he was terrified of my power to hurt him and was settling for a safe, cosy alternative. I nearly went mad with grief, and spent my time either crying or writing him long letters which were never answered. I had never felt so lonely in my life.

My only admirer at the time was a strange Ceylonese poet called Tambimuttu, who had black floppy hair, a gap in his front teeth and long prehensile fingers that curved outwards. He was in love with me and wanted us to get married and have lots of coffee-coloured children.

One night, at the Hog in the Pound, off Oxford Street, he disappeared for a while and came back bearing a Woolworths' engagement ring set with three imitation opals. Unfortunately, when I went to wash my hands in the ladies' room, all the stones came loose and went tinkling down the plughole, leaving nothing behind but a sort of wire mesh. I was so embarrassed and so terrified of hurting poor Tambi's feelings that I sneaked out through the back entrance and never came back.

The next day a beautiful poem was delivered by hand. After lots of nonsense about my golden hair etc. – my hair is brown – he went on:

> Not too reckless when you go to the greyhounds
> And not too hasty when you choose a man,
> With level eyes and heart you take the fences
> Like Golden Miller, easily at the jumps;
> And I think you've narrowed all your fancies
> Underneath the mind's glittering lenses.

I had never been to bed with Tambi. He once lured me to his room, but when he stripped back the sheets there were bed bugs, so I ran away.

*

It was New Year's Eve, 1946, and I began to get over Kit, and to feel more hopeful. It was snowing, and snow always brings me luck. Tambi rang up and said he was going to take me to a very interesting party in Hampstead given by the poet William Empson.

It was a big, old-fashioned Bohemian sort of house, and the party was going on in an upstairs room with a bar running right across it. I was wondering whether to get sloshed when I noticed a boy watching me from the other side of the room. He was thin and hawklike with hair growing low on his forehead and eyes that darted furtively from side to side. Eventually he came up to me and told me he was called Lucian Freud. After we had talked for a long time he opened a trap door in the floor and took me down some rickety stairs to a nursery where Empson's children were sleeping. He pushed me back against Mogador's cot and kissed me, but Empson came down in a great rage and shooed us up again. Lucian said, 'Let's get out of here', so I gave Tambi the slip, and we sloshed our way back through the snow to Lucian's studio.

It was freezing cold, and there was a funny sort of smell. I finally tracked this down to a rather depressed-looking hawk who was sitting on the floor of his cage pecking at the remains of a very dead mouse. I have to admit that Lucian made me feel slightly uncomfortable – he was so twitchy, and generated such an intense nervous energy.

We went to bed, but because I was still mourning after Kit, I felt hardly any lust at all. What I really wanted, I suppose, was a new interest, something to distract me, or maybe even just company. In an icy bed I made love to an intriguing mind and a finely chiselled face, but no more.

Next morning Lucian spent hours drawing the hawk, which looked just like him. Every filament on every feather was meticulously recorded – he seemed to be dissecting his subject rather than drawing it. There were paintings of women round the room which I thought were very good but a bit dead-looking, like butterflies pinned to the canvas.

Because Lucian's whole attention was concentrated on his work I began to feel a bit unwanted and got up to go, but he said he would come with me as he had friends to visit. He put on a long black coat, very old and rusty-looking, with a fur collar – he said it had belonged to his grandfather, Sigmund Freud. Then, to my amazement, he opened the hawk's cage and fastened the reluctant bird to his wrist with a thong.

'You're not going to take that thing on the Tube, are you?' I asked in alarm. 'Of course,' Lucian said: 'I'm training it to go everywhere with me.' Going down the escalator to the Northern Line the hawk rose in the air and started squawking and flapping its wings, much to the alarm of the other travellers. It didn't seem to like Lucian very much.

During the next few weeks I went around a lot with Lucian and his friend Johnny Craxton, his inseparable companion. I think I was a little bit in love with Johnny, he was so tall and lovely-looking, not at all threatening or dangerous like Lucian. Unfortunately it wasn't any good as he only thought of me as Lucian's girl. We went to concerts in the Chelsea Town Hall and to incomprehensible arty plays like *Desire Caught by the Tail*, by Picasso, and picked up funny old second-hand clothes in East End markets. Johnny got a splendid admiral's greatcoat which he wore with seamen's boots.

Life with Lucian was never easy, as he was so unpredictable. One day he promised to meet me at the Café Royal at seven and I sat in the foyer for nearly an hour watching that wretched swing-door going round and round till I was almost in an hypnotic trance. I longed to go upstairs and spend a penny but didn't dare in case I missed him. When he finally arrived he said nothing at all about being late, just took me through to the back bar which was then *the* place where smart people went. I got off with one of the managers of Butlin's Holiday Camp, who tried to recruit me for a Redcoat. He was awfully nice but Lucian didn't seem at all amused.

A new twist to our relationship. We were in bed when a girl's voice said 'Cuppa tea, love?' and I saw this dark girl with huge eyes who totally ignored me and didn't offer me any tea. The next two nights she slept on the sofa, but I had a curious premonition that it wouldn't be long before I was on the sofa and she was in the bed. I think her name was Kitty. Before long it became obvious that Lucian wanted to get rid of me.

He made a little speech about his attitude to sex. Apparently he is scared of serious relationships. What he really liked, he said, was to pick up unknown little girls in the park and bring them home like stray kittens. I wondered whether Kitty had once been a stray kitten – if so she was showing remarkable signs of domesticity, and getting her paws well and truly under the table. I didn't really believe him, but I got the message loud and clear. One thing I liked about Lucian was that he always told me the truth, no matter how painful.

I decided to run away from London and Lucian as soon as possible, and by a fortunate coincidence Veronica's niece Joy – who was my great friend – had been caught having an affair with V.'s young lover, so she was also longing to do a bolt. We decided to hitchhike to the Scilly Isles, which was the farthest place from London we could think of.

I fished out my old WAAF trousers, the ones I used to wear on night duty, and bought a knapsack and a very rakish red beret into which I stuffed my hair. Joy also dressed as a boy, and was carrying her Siamese cat in a cardboard box.

We got a lorry as far as Taunton where we slept in a hay rick – very itchy – and during the night the cat ran away and was never found. We made St Ives by the following day, and holed up in the local artist Sven Berlin's tower for a couple of nights.

There was a tiny plane that went to the Scilly Isles, piloted by a very eccentric but nice young man who said we could stay with him there. He had a film projector in his bedroom and stacks of old films (which are his passion) so we spent our first evening on the island watching *The Cabinet of Doctor Caligari*. Afterwards he took us to the docks where brawny fishermen were tossing live crabs into vats of hissing water by the light of storm lanterns.

Next day we set out to explore the town, which is called Hugh Town. We were sitting outside a café drinking tea when a very old and battered open car pulled up outside, full of young French boys and girls wearing black sweaters and trousers and carrying guitars. The boys had beards and the girls had long, straight hair. They said they were Existentialists from Paris, and that they were living just down the coast in a cave. Apparently there was lots of room and we could stay with them if we liked. Joy looked a bit doubtful, but I was frantic with curiosity, so we piled into their car and headed for the coast.

It was a huge cave, with rocky shelves for sitting and sleeping on, piles of dried seaweed for bedding, and a soft, sandy floor where little transparent crabs scuttled. A driftwood fire was smoking in the centre. A very tall, serious-looking girl called Monique took a piece of flat corrugated iron and laid it over the fire. When it was red hot she sprinkled some limpets on top. This, I gathered, was lunch. The poor limpets sizzled and spurted in their own juices, and as they cooked their little black eyes shot out on stalks – most unpleasant. While we were chewing the fishy-tasting pieces of rubber, Monique's lover Pierre played us sad songs by Mouloudji on his guitar. The other boy, Pepé, was a painter and had set his canvas up by the mouth of the cave. His masterpiece was 'St Anne's Sans Culottes', which showed the main square of the town with all the local bigwigs suddenly losing their trousers. When he was not painting, Pepé fixed his toffee-brown eyes lecherously on me and Joy. I feared he had designs on us.

Joy and I were just thinking of sneaking off in search of a fish and chip shop when Pierre sauntered in carrying a home-made catapult in one hand and, in the other, a dead seagull and a bunch of wild garlic. 'On bouffe bien ce soir!' he announced cheerfully, flinging us the seagull to pluck and gut. Both operations were extremely nasty and difficult, and after all that hard work it tasted mainly of rancid, oily fish. But worse was to come. Joy and I were lying on our seaweed bed, wracked with cold and indigestion, when Pepé decided to make his move. Suddenly, a small, wiry, brown body landed on top of us, full of lustful expectation, and obviously not particularly worried as to which of us he got. Luckily we were strong girls, and threw him off.

Next morning, we explained our dilemma to Pierre and Monique, who came up with an excellent solution. A few hundred yards away, on the summit of the cliff, there was an early Anglo-Saxon tomb, or barrow, which previous occupants had converted into a comfortable home. It was just big enough for two, with shelves for our gear and plenty of dried leaves to sleep on – much better than smelly seaweed. Next day, apparently miffed by our refusal, Pepé left the cave, having stolen all my clothing coupons and my beautiful Shetland sweater.

For a time we were very happy in our new home, waking to the cries of wheeling gulls and the pale light lifting over the distant seas. Everything had such purity of shape there – every rock, pebble and shell was perfect. Crawling out of the barrow we could smell crushed thyme, and before us was a path strewn with empty white snail shells and turf studded with small, pink flowers like pincushions, with matching pink and green beetles sitting on them. Pierre brought us a rabbit he had snared and we cooked it over a fire in the open air, flavoured with thyme and wild garlic – it was delicious.

I could happily have stayed there for weeks, but fate was against us. Two days later we were woken at dawn by the sound of strange, rough voices. Peering through the round entrance to our barrow, we saw, outlined against the grey morning light, two pairs of dark trousers ending in outsize boots. The local police had come to evict us. Down below on the beach we could see Pierre and Monique being driven from their cave carrying knapsacks and guitars.

'We don't like your sort 'ere!' a constable told us; and ordered us to go immediately to Penzance on the mainland and report to the police station as vagrants. Luckily they were very nice to us there, and let us go with a caution.

Not wanting to return to London, I thought I might look up my Dad, who had a beautiful house near Uckfield called Tickerage Mill, with a cottage in the grounds. Although I hardly knew my father, and was, in fact, slightly in awe of him, I felt sure he would be delighted to see me – but, as things turned out it wasn't that simple.

After hitching half across England, we arrived at Tickerage after dark. As we were trudging wearily up the lane towards the Mill, a tousled figure shot up from behind a hedge, his arms around the neck of a small horse. His eyes were rolling madly, contorting one side of his face into a hideous leer. 'Ah-hargh!' hissed the apparition. 'And who might you be, me beauties?'

Gosh, I thought, it's Long John Silver – nobody else rolled his eyes and said 'Ah-hargh!' quite like that! But what on earth was the film actor Robert Newton, last seen in *Treasure Island*, doing in a field with a horse in the middle of the night?

'We're looking for my father,' I said. 'Have you any idea where he is?'

'I certainly do,' said Newton. 'He's run off with my wife to Monte Carlo, so I'm sleeping with my horse. I love my horse,' he added, 'and hate the human race, but as you've obviously got nowhere to go you'd better come back to my place.'

This turned out to be a small cottage with one huge bed. But we needn't have worried – Bobby Newton finished off the remaining two-thirds of a bottle of whisky and passed out unconscious in the middle of the bed, with Joy and I lying fully clothed and rigid on either side of him.

After a few pleasant days spent spinning around the countryside in his pony trap, with Bobby waving his whip in the air and swigging from a whisky flask, he announced he was in love with me. Needless to say nothing had happened between us, but it was quite a relief when I finally saw the lights go on in Tickerage Mill. Joy left for London, and with some trepidation I found my way to the big house.

The housekeeper let me in. No, the Major was not back yet but was expected this evening. Would I like to wait in the drawing-room? Mr Quennell was there, and Mr Harcourt-Smith, and, surprisingly, Mrs Newton, back from Monte Carlo. I was terrified. I loved my father dearly and only wished I saw more of him, but I simply couldn't cope with his smart friends who made me feel so clumsy and naive.

I opened the drawing-room door quietly and went in. Three people were sitting round the fireplace discussing bad taste in the cinema. I heard the phrase 'Spoon-fed with bollocks!' from a winged chair in the corner. 'My dear Nat, what a quaint expression!' said a beautiful blond man. Then they saw me and all conversation stopped. They obviously hadn't a clue who I was. However the penny must have dropped, for someone said enquiringly, 'Dick's daughter?' and the lady in the chair swivelled to look at me. She was the ultimate bitch-goddess, smart and skinny, with big slanting cats' eyes, and bent on my destruction.

'My God!' she snarled. 'So *you're* the little tart who's been sleeping with Bobby! Well, darling, it's not *all that difficult* to sleep with Bobby, you know! I daresay any girl who lay down in the middle of Piccadilly Circus and waved her legs in the air could get Bobby – he's not particularly fussy.'

'But you don't understand,' I stammered. 'It wasn't an affair or anything like that!' I could feel my legs shaking as I ploughed on disastrously, saying, as I often do in these situations, the worst and most embarrassing thing possible. 'You see,' I said, 'it's not that I'm interested in *Bobby*, I'm just fascinated by the cinema!'

'The *cinemah*!' she screeched, laughing so much she could hardly speak. 'Simon, Peter, did you *hear* that? This dear little creature is interested in the *cinemah*! I suppose you'll be telling me next that you think Bobby is a genius and it's your mission in life to get him off the booze?'

As I was standing there, feeling ready to sink through the floor with embarrassment, the man called Peter cried warningly, 'Watch out, Nat, I can hear Dick coming!'

He came in, tall, shambling and myopic, did a doubletake on me and finally realised I was his daughter. Then it was all big hugs and kisses and cries of 'Joanie, darling!' It was like the end of one of those Greek tragedies when a god comes down from Olympus to make everything all right. Natalie said nothing, but watched us both through half-shut eyes.

Dick lumbered off to the cellar to choose wines for dinner and the two men – Peter Quennell and Simon Harcourt-Smith – became suddenly all charm and friendliness. In spite of Nat I now felt that I 'belonged'.

I was put to sleep in a little room that led into my father's bedroom, and for the first two nights I was woken in the early hours by a slim figure in white pyjamas tiptoeing through my room towards the master bedroom, and by Natalie's gloating voice saying 'Hello, Joanie, I'm going to sleep with your *daddy*!' After a couple of days, however, she went back to Bobby, and soon after I decided to return to London.

A quick scan of the visitors' book as I left showed that Peter Quennell had written 'Unexpected arrival of Dick's daughter, Joan Olivia, old enough to be his daughter but young and pretty enough to be his mistress.' I was glad to leave. It was all rather more than I could cope with.

Back in Cadogan Street I found two telegrams awaiting me.

'Have been trying to contact you for days because I miss you so much. Please darling ring me Welwyn Garden 3241 any time. All my love Bobby.' The other one said simply 'Marry me darling and I'll only drink one bottle a day.' We spent a few chaste nights together, my only job being to get him to the studio next morning sober and on time. However the final straw came when we went to the Gargoyle Club – Bobby on crutches after a drunken fall – to be confronted by Natalie, who was sitting drinking with Dylan Thomas. A half empty bottle of Chablis hurtled towards my head, but was ably fended off by one of the Bobby's crutches. As Dylan forcibly restrained Natalie from attacking me with her nails, I ran off, leaving Bobby to his fate, and managed to make the small rickety lift down to Soho and safety.

Chapter Two

A few weeks later I got a 'phone call from a friend in Oxford saying there was a big party on the following Saturday and would I come. I had always wanted to see Oxford again, and accepted with alacrity. It was given in a Walton Street flat by a tall, good-looking man with blond floppy hair. He was called Maurice Rowdon and was taking a post-war degree at Keble. We took one look at each other and spent the rest of the night talking and dancing. A few days later I moved in with him.

Oxford in 1947 was a very exciting place to be, full of older students who'd been through the war, but the glittering star was undoubtedly young Ken Tynan with his bony face, pale hair and prominent teeth, stalking the streets in his green and purple suits and followed by a swarm of sycophants and hangers-on. Maurice and I both loved and hated him, for one day he would be nice to you and the next he would treat you like dirt. I first met him sitting by his side on the floor at some party. He asked Maurice 'Who is this wonderful girl who gives out such warmth? It's like sitting next to a little primus stove,' after which he spent a long time deep in conversation with him. But only two nights later, at a party on a college barge, when Maurice greeted him with 'Hello, Ken' he snarled 'How I *loathe* people who call me Ken in that sycophantic fashion!' Maurice, paranoid at the best of times, was deeply hurt, and we never forgave Ken for letting adulation spoil him so.

Meanwhile in our little flat in Walton Street I studied short-hand and typing, Mo wrote his thesis, and we both kept fancy mice. These mice were my passion. They came from our path-ologist friend Donald Michie's laboratory, and were not just ordinary brown mice but lavender, cinnamon, mink, pink cham-pagne, piebald and albino. Twenty cages were piled up one on top of another in our kitchen, full of madly copulating mice who produced multi-coloured offspring. The overflow went straight back to Donald's lab. There was one unfortunate occasion when Michael Foot came to tea and left in a huff because he strongly objected to piebald mice running around the table and nibbling at his anchovy toast.

After we had been together for a few months, Maurice decided it was time to introduce me to his family, a lovely working-class couple who lived in Garratt Lane, Wandsworth. With iron determination, Mo's mother, who was unable to read or write, had seen three sons through public school and university. His father, Old Bill, was an ex-docker with an iron hook for a hand. There was a front parlour that was never used, and life revolved around the kitchen with its ever-warm teapot. We stayed there a lot and I felt enormously safe and happy with them.

In March I discovered I was pregnant, and although it had been an accident we were delighted, and decided to get married. The only snag was that Mo would have to become a Roman Catholic – but as he had no religious feelings at all he readily agreed, thinking it all a bit of a joke. As for me, I had almost totally lost my faith over the last few years. The concentration camps were still fresh in my mind, and in particular the suffering of children. Like Alyosha in *The Brothers Karamazov*, I felt that the world's salvation was not worth the suffering of one innocent child, and had 'respectfully handed back my ticket'. But we had to go through with it for the sake of my Mum, who still believed me to be a fervent Catholic.

The unfortunate Maurice was sent for indoctrination to the celebrated Father D'Arcy, a 'pezzo pezzante' of the Jesuit order. Mo soon got bogged down on original sin, and there were long sessions over Earl Grey tea and buttered scones. Father D'Arcy trotted out all those arguments I remembered from my convent days – 'No sun without shade, no good without the choice of evil', and so on. 'But why not a choice between good and *better*,' Maurice asked, genuinely puzzled: 'I mean, here's God, all-good and all-powerful – with all eternity to plan it in, how did he come up with such a monumental cock-up as the human race?'

Father D'Arcy was patient and persistent, but he had met his match. The upshot was that my daughter Clare beat Mo to the baptismal font by three weeks.

I was visited in the nursing-home by my father, who had some difficulty in finding me as he had forgotten my name. He was wearing a sheepskin coat down to his ankles and walking on crutches. Apparently he had crashed his plane in the mountains of Persia and walked hundreds of miles to the nearest village, living on sunflower seeds and suffering from frostbite. It was the last time I ever saw him.

I was married a few weeks later, gliding down the aisle in my best grey two-piece and hat with veil, to the strains of 'Greensleeves'. Old Bill gave me away, looking amazingly smart – 'all dolled up like a talleyman's ink bottle', as he proudly put it. Immediately after the ceremony I had to hare back to Nell Gwynn House to breast-feed the baby.

That evening there was a slap-up party with his parents in Garratt Lane, with lots of sparkling wine and funny hats. We danced and did 'Knees Up Mother Brown', and all the fattest ladies linked arms for a song called 'Bobbing Up and Down Like This', their huge bosoms bouncing in unison. Uncle George sang his party piece, a music hall song called 'My Old Watch'. It was a smashing do.

In 1948 I still had one more term to go at the Oxford secretarial school, so we moved to an old college barge on the river. It was an idyllic period. In the morning we would watch the swans taking off with a noise like torn silk, and then Mo would get out the dinghy and row downstream for the milk, towing me behind him on a rope. Every Sunday I read my father's despatches from the Middle East where he was covering the Arab–Israeli war for the *Sunday Times*, and thought how lovely it would be to take Clare down to Tickerage Mill and show her to him.

One normal, happy Sunday in May I was sitting on the closed loo seat reading bits of the paper out to Maurice who was soaping himself in the bath, when I was struck dumb by the following words: 'Dick Wyndham was killed on Wednesday morning outside Jerusalem.' Apparently he had stood on the skyline to get a photograph dressed up in Arab Legion uniform, and had been cut down by a sniper's bullet from the Hadassah Hospital. Ian Fleming went on to describe him as one of the great bohemians of his age. He saw in his 'insolent but gentle brilliance those qualities of panache and chivalry which are the inheritance of great Englishmen'. Silly old sod, I thought, he always did like dressing up.

As always after the death of someone close, one's feelings were divided between sorrow and cupidity – what had he left in his will? I felt terrible – one-dimensional, as if half my being had gone missing – but both Maurice and I must have had a sneaking suspicion that we were now very rich. This illusion was short-lived. What with his private aeroplane, his vast cellar and his mistresses, my father had run up enormous debts, and practically everything had to be sold to meet the death duties.

I finished my secretarial course and Maurice sat for his finals. On our last day we had tea and pancakes at Kemp's Café with Mo's friend Kingsley Amis. 'What are you going to do now, Kingsley?' Maurice asked. Kingsley went into paroxysms of mock embarrassment and horror, practically falling off his chair. 'Write, I suppose!' he finally spluttered. 'Me too,' said Maurice gloomily, helping himself to some more pancakes.

When my father's estate was finally settled we had just enough money to buy a small, whitewashed cottage in Shoreham, a beautiful old village in Kent, and we moved in with our baby Clare. Domesticity – how I hated it! Much as I loved my daughter, I wasn't too keen on the rest of the stuff that goes with motherhood. Those were the days when nappies were soaked in pails, boiled up on top of the stove and hung out to dry in the garden. In spite of rationing I cooked a huge fantastic meal twice a day, and grew fat and ugly. We had a rabbit who lived behind the stove, a deaf white cat, and an allotment. There I grew nothing as common as cabbages, but only the most exotic things like blue cocoa beans, mangetout peas, ornamental gourds and Mediterranean herbs.

I had a pleasant house in one of the prettiest villages in Kent, an adoring husband and a lovely daughter – so why was I so bloody miserable? One reason, I suppose, was the hostility of the natives, who ignored us totally. Only two families befriended us – the author Lord Dunsany and his wife, who had the big house on the hill, and were both very grand and very eccentric, and a couple known to the village as 'the Communists' because of their mildly liberal views.

I longed for bright city lights, society and entertainment, and filled my empty days with cooking and gardening. I hoed and mulched, pickled and preserved, but all the time I was dreaming of Negro nightclubs, young bearded boys in tight black trousers, and smart literary parties full of my father's old friends.

They were all there at his memorial service, but no one spoke to me except for Lys Connolly who said 'What a pretty hat' – to which I replied, rather feebly, that I had made it myself.

Afterwards Maurice and I stood on the church steps watching the people come out. Everybody knew everybody else and they were all rushing off to private lunches and drinks, so after Mo and I had stood around feeling stupid for about half an hour, we said 'Sod it' and went off to the nearest pub to get drunk.

The chip on my shoulder was now assuming tree-like pro-portions. It grew even bigger after a visit to the butcher's one day in search of unrationed meat. I was not tempted by something hanging up that looked like a skinned dwarf, and turned out to be a badger, so took home a big package of offal wrapped up in newspaper. As I peeled off the outer covering, sticky with pigs' blood, I could just make out an entry in the social column: a coming-out party for my half-sister, Miss Ingrid Wyndham, with a marquee specially designed by Oliver Messel. The guest list which followed included many of my father's friends and relatives, and even the now socially ubiqui-tous Lucian Freud. All this was fuel to my increasing paranoia, and the feeling that the death of my father had cut me off from everything interesting in life. Ingrid had been brought up quite differently by my step-grandmother, the madly worldly and witty Violet Wyndham, and inhabited a world of parties and dances where one met 'the right people'.

I was sitting in my bedroom brooding when Maurice burst in, wildly excited because Heinemann had accepted his first novel. It was called *Hellebore the Clown* – Hell-of-a-bore the Clown to his more cynical friends. I thought it was rather a good book, in spite of such gaffes as having Hellebore open champagne with a corkscrew.

To help supplement our income I started going to the greyhound races again, and indoctrinated Mo. We went to the dogs twice a week and played the forecasts. I had graphs of all the tracks pinned up on my bedroom wall, and used a variety of complicated systems. Sometimes we made a killing, but on the whole C. Edgar, our bookie, did rather better.

We also took a lodger, our friend James Michie from Oxford, who was popularly supposed to be the original for Lucky Jim. As a conscientious objector he had chosen to do farm work instead of National Service, and was lucky enough to be working for our friends 'the Communists'.

One day I made the mistake of sending him to collect the coal in the baby's pram, and he was later observed by the villagers kicking the pram downhill while he chased after it, whooping and gibbering. Three days later we got a call from the NSPCC claiming that we were housing a baby batterer.

Altogether we weren't going down too well with the villagers, so I was quite excited to get a 'phone call from Cyril Connolly asking us to come up to London and meet him for lunch in Soho. Apparently he had a big trunk of my father's papers for me to go through.

What on earth should we wear? I went to my 'little woman' in the village and collected a new two-piece in blue tweed that I had ordered from a pattern. The material seemed very stiff, like cardboard, and the skirt stuck out in an unflattering way. Maurice had a choice between his jumble-sale duffle coat – very grubby – or a present from his Dad, an Acton Park Divisional Inspector of Railways mackintosh. It was black, large and shiny and made him look like a Gestapo agent. It was snowing heavily. On my way to the station I met a boy who persuaded me to slide down Hunter's Hill on his toboggan. Needless to say I fell off, and arrived at the Etoile wearing a suit that was not only badly cut, but also soaking wet.

Cyril Connolly, who had already started to eat – he was both rude *and* greedy – looked up from his plovers' eggs and eyed me without enthusiasm. I was introduced to his assistant, Sonia Brownell, who was later to marry George Orwell. She was wearing something impeccable by Chanel with a white ruffled shirt, and managed to look both sexy and intelligent. Maurice arrived, and I hoped he would behave himself and not go off on one of his left-wing rampages. Actually Cyril seemed more interested in his lunch and in his incredible luck at getting the first plovers' eggs of the season. Sonia at least made an effort.

'This trunk-load of letters,' she said, smiling at me. 'We found it when we went down to Tickerage to hide the whips.'

I looked bemused.

Cyril's pudgy face lit up with malice. 'But, my dear,' he said, 'didn't you *know* that your father was one of Europe's most famous flagellists?' I replied feebly that I'd no idea.

'Well, he wasn't called Whips Wyndham for nothing, was he?' put in Sonia. 'I remember one famous house party when the lady guests spent most of their time *up trees!*' I was beginning to feel thoroughly uncomfortable and out of my depth, the way I had with Nat Newton at Tickerage, and it was a relief when we went back to Sussex Place, where Cyril then lived.

Cyril plonked a trunkful of letters down in front of me and suddenly developed a fearful cold. It was, he said, absolutely essential that he went straight to bed – the maid would bring us tea – '*So* nice seeing you – goodbye!' He hadn't seemed at all ill when he was scoffing his plovers' eggs, so I supposed he just didn't like us very much.

Soon after this rather dispiriting little meeting, I discovered I was pregnant again, which cheered me up no end. We decided to take a holiday in France and Austria, and my mother moved in to look after Clare. I had hoped for a nice comfortable hotel in the Alps, but Maurice said he had to stay with 'real people' – which meant, I imagined, some primitive peasant's hut up a steep goat track. But first we had a few days in Paris – and being free of domestic responsibilities I was able to start up my diary again.

* *

Thursday, 3 May 1956. How wonderful after Shoreham! We are in St Germain des Prés, the place I dreamt of while my frostbitten fingers were picking sprouts in the allotment. The sights and sounds of the quarter are completely intoxicating – a wild exuberance without formal pattern, uninhibited people, magnificently odorous food shops and café tables crowded in the spring sun. In the market there are stalls piled high with live snails and crabs, wine is two shillings a bottle and you can carry fresh cream back to the hotel in your toothglass. Tonight we are going to the Opéra to see Kirsten Flagstad's farewell performance as Isolde.

Friday, 4 May. Explored the Latin quarter, which makes Chelsea seem tame. Never have I seen so many beards and black trousers! To be an Existentialist, it is apparently essential to wear black – presumably because it doesn't show the dirt. Mo's Acton Town Divisional Inspector of Railways mac has found its true home at last.

In the evenings beebop and jazz flourish. Tight black trousers, sleeveless black tops, Greek sandals and long, straight hair like seaweed are *de rigueur*. I have bought myself a black maternity shirt to dance in.

Saturday, 5 May. To the Harlequin Club, a cellar where Mouloudji sings sentimental songs by Prévost and Cosma. Later a Negro began to belt out jazz and I watched the gyrating girls enviously. I had dreamt of this so often, but this was the first time I had actually seen them *doing* it! What sequence of steps were they following? How did they know what to do with their feet? I was sitting with a strained smile of phoney participation on my face when a big Negro stopped in front of me, extending the dry map of his hand. I clung on to it desperately and was dragged into the sea of dancers. To my wonder and surprise I find myself following him – I could do it!

Sunday, 6 May. James Michie joined us, sporting a terrible ginger backwoodsman's beard bushier on one side than the other. I think he knows he looks awful and is in a terrible mood. Lunch with Lucian's old friend the painter Johnny Craxton at the Oriental, a wonderful students' café where a portion of spit-roasted suckling lamb with rice costs half a crown. Johnny shows off and name-drops, and James hates him.

Tuesday, 8 May. We are now in Austria, and Frau Elmer's farmhouse is just as primitive and just as isolated as I had feared. Jolting up the steep mountain road I felt pains in my stomach and lost some blood. The village doctor has given me an injection.

Next morning, waking to clear blue skies and white flowering fruit trees, I felt better, more hopeful. The doctor has said he thinks the child will live. All around us are fields of wild crocus, gentian, cowslip and anenomes. We sleep in a huge white feather bed under a hideous oil painting of Christ at Gethsemane.

The farm belongs to Frau Elmer, a tiny gypsy-like woman with a tongue like a viper. She lives with her illegitimate son and daughter, plus her legitimate daughter and the daughter's illegitimate son by an American. The first sight of the 'abort' – what a ghastly word! – which we appear to share with the cows, has succeeded in constipating me for four days.

The real life of the farm goes on in the communal kitchen, where something is always simmering or baking, where butter is churned and bread kneaded. There is always a huge crowd of people – babies rolling on the dusty floor, young men with concertinas, old men drunk on schnapps, dogs begging and women mending, cooking and gossiping. Every Saturday, a drunken party goes on until dawn.

They work incredibly hard from 5 a.m. to 8.30 at night, and all day the kitchen smells comfortingly of hot tea liberally dosed with apple schnapps. Without it they could never keep going. I help with the butter churning and bread-making – at first I used to pick out the weevils, whose legs I could see waving, but I soon gave it up as a bad job.

Because Maurice and I are paying guests we get given wonderful food, rich and primitive – beef in thick gravy with caraway seeds, veal fried in egg and breadcrumbs, and heavy pancakes eaten with butter and homemade honey, which unfortunately is always full of ants. The family, on the other hand, rarely eat fresh meat or vegetables, but every possible combination of milk, flour, butter and eggs, with an occasional slice hacked from the bacon that hangs from the rafters. On feast days they will roast a kid and eat it with garlic dumplings, followed by yeast cakes as heavy as depth charges which they drop into boiling fat. All this is washed down with lashings of tea and strong fragrant schnapps, homemade from apples or 'bird berries'.

Tuesday, 15 May. Today I climbed 1,000 feet to the snowline and still feel fine. No one here believes that I'm twenty-nine – they are very pleased at my lack of lipstick and nail varnish, unlike American women who, says Frau Elmer with gross pantomime, put red paint even on their bottoms and other unmentionable places. Today at breakfast she asked Maurice, 'Is it true that all Englishmen use powder and rouge?' Mo and I try hard to make conversation, but we have a very outdated AA phrase book containing such gems as 'Please use the curling tongs for my moustache,' 'Is that Mr Strauss playing now?' and 'Please can you give me six very high collars and an opera hat.'

Next door we can hear the father of Frau Elmer's illegitimate children singing Tyrolean folk songs. He and his family are all sitting round a big scrubbed table with an iron pot of rice topped with jam in the middle of it. Each member is armed with a spoon and they set to at a given signal – every man for himself, except that the oldest has the right to scrape the burnt bits off the bottom.

The women eat separately, in a mood of Rabelaisian mirth, egging each other on to further flights of obscenity at the expense of some wretched man's physical shortcomings. They slap their thighs and laugh till tears run down their cheeks. Frau Elmer's favourite proverb: 'A cock can fart but it can't lay eggs'.

Our last day. It is also Mutterstag, so the daughters have put on their dirndls and washed their feet in honour of the occasion.

Thursday, 24 May. Two and six a night at the Stein Gasse guest house in Salzburg, which is all red marble with holy water stoups. There are so many pleasures here – the castle by moonlight, zither music in dark cellars, raspberry ices with whipped cream. Maurice drags me to endless chamber music concerts: nothing makes the bones come through my bottom sooner than a string quartet, but he is remorseless. Because of all this culture we can only afford to eat hot frankfurters from stalls in the street.

Tuesday, 29 May. A violin concert in the white and gold salon of the Mozarteum. In the middle of the slow movement of Brahms's violin concerto I began to have terrible pains and to lose blood. Mo rushed me home and called a doctor, a tall, sad-looking man. While the doctor was examining me Mo went out to buy some sausages, and came back in time to hear the doctor say in his slow, grave voice 'Das kind ist nicht'. It had been dead for two months.

The state-run hospital in Salzburg where I went for my operation costs five shillings a day. There is a water tap in the corner of the ward and nothing to eat except black bread with ersatz coffee. Visiting hours are one long banqueting procession of relatives bearing delicatessen. On one side of me is a peasant woman with fourteen children, on the other a young Jewish girl who washes herself compulsively all day long. Maurice brings me wild strawberries and we play word games. The doctors are very kind and competent. When they told me I had lost a boy I cried and cried. As a result of this tragedy we have finally decided to leave Shoreham and to move to a flat in London.

5 Redcliffe Gardens: July 1951. The first few weeks in the London flat have been wonderful – people in and out night and day, the spare bedroom never vacant, and everybody eating in the kitchen and drinking Entre Deux Mers at five shillings a bottle. Maurice is busy writing his second novel while I cook endless noodle casseroles.

Upstairs two spades called Ted and Chico live in a permanent cloud of marijuana smoke. They lie all day in front of the gas fire, rolled in sleeping bags with their hats on. Their conversation is minimal:

TED: Man, that's a cool fire!

CHICO: Gotta spliff, man?
TED: Pick it up, daddio.

Five spliffs cost one pound, and are called a 'tula'. When
Ted rolls his own they are so big they stand on end like little
rockets. Needless to say they are always being stopped in the
street by the police, but, as Ted says proudly, 'They got
nothing on me, man – they just don't like the way I wave
around!'

On Friday nights they commandeer the bathroom, where,
amid clouds of steam, they can be seen upright in the bath,
treading their dirty laundry to a calypso beat.

Downstairs are two dodgy second-hand car dealers, who
never answer the door or accept registered letters. To avoid
paying bills they have broken the seal and 'hot-lined' the
electricity with some complicated system involving a cork and
a needle which short-circuits the wires. They specialise in
'bangers' whose brake linings have been stuffed with sawdust
or silk stockings, and are constantly getting irate phone calls
threatening to take their legs off at the knee. There was one
yesterday from a furious chap who'd bought an old Austin
Seven – the bottom fell out and he found himself running
down Shaftesbury Avenue at thirty miles an hour, still holding
on to the steering wheel.

Sometimes at weekends they take Ted and Chico out for a
spin in their big Sedanka de Ville. '*High* Wycombe, man!'
Ted screeches as they roar through the Bucks countryside
waving their spliffs.

The letter that was to change our lives arrived in late summer, just
as I was beginning to tire a little of London. There was a vacancy
for an English teacher at the Queen Aliyah College in Baghdad.
Maurice would go ahead to find a house and Clare and I would
follow. I looked at the grey day outside and a golden image glowed
in my head of domes and minarets, teeming bazaars, wild-eyed
sheikhs mounted on camels – I don't think we hesitated for more
than a moment. I now had to think about letting our flat, and was
told of a 'very nice chap' who was looking for somewhere cheap
to live with his girlfriend.

Sunday, 2 September. Arrival of Shura Shivarg, the 'very nice chap – in fact a faintly dangerous-looking but undoubtedly attractive Russian in one of those macs that private dicks wear in the films. He had been brought up in China before coming to England to take up an Oxford grant, and speaks perfect English, Russian and Chinese.

Calmly ignoring my daughter, who was sitting on her potty in front of a miniature easel, painting a portrait of her teddy bear, he set out to impress me. In the course of one hour he had showed me how to make aubergine caviar, taught me the Chinese ideogram for a brothel, sung a couple of wild Russian gypsy songs, and translated Rimbaud's 'Bâteau Ivre' impromptu into rhyming English. A man of many parts I thought, feeling slightly stunned – so stunned in fact that I let him have the flat immediately without even enquiring about his financial status. However he struck me as being very reliable and his girlfriend, Bianca, appeared to be dead respectable so I would probably get the rent. ❧

Chapter Three

N‍*Tuesday, 25 September 1951.* To Marseilles in a heat
wave to catch our boat to Beirut. Although only three,
Clare seems to have turned into a mature and helpful adult
overnight. She adores the travelling, and blue-chinned porters
and sinister matelots melt like butter at her approach. No
tears, no tantrums – I fear it's too good to last.

My fears were unfounded – after a trouble-free voyage the
boat finally docked and was met by a villainous crew lined up
on the quayside like a chorus from *The Beggars' Opera* –
luckily they had 'Cook's' written on their chests, so all was
well.

Beirut is how I imagine Elizabethan England must have
been, filthy but exciting, and full of evil but enthralling smells.
The streets are thronged with hawkers, singers, whores,
beggars and gypsies; everywhere people are arguing, fighting
or cooking on the pavement.

Clare and I are here to be inoculated against the dreaded
'Baghdad boil', a pustule that leaves a huge crater in your
face. Apparently half the population of Baghdad have suffered
from it!

Friday, 5 October. A long haul on the desert bus to Baghdad,
stopping off at Damascus to be sick.

Maurice met the bus and we drove through town to the River Front Hotel. My dreams of a glamorous life began to fade. The town is tatty and ugly, and very modern except for a few malodorous back alleys. Outside our hotel bedroom kites hover and peasants appear to be washing carpets in the hotel sewage.

In the bar the waiters bring round little trays of shrivelled chicken livers and call me 'memsahib'. Me, a memsahib?

After dinner we went for a walk in the town and saw the desert people lounging in the coffee shop in their huge cloaks, smoking hubble-bubbles, fanning themselves with palm leaves and playing with their beads. Arabs have a curious effect on me – they make me feel deeply despised for being a woman, yet very sexy and feminine at the same time, I don't know why!

Desmond Stewart, a lovely, intelligent queen who also works at the college, has found us a large, beautiful house in El Waziriyah, a quiet leafy suburb of white houses and eucalyptus trees. Inside the house the walls are pale green with rose-red fireplaces.

Wednesday, 10 October. The first thing I see when I wake up in the morning is a pale, almost transparent lizard, immobile on the wall above my bed. Then – because my bed is on the floor – come the brown boots of Abed, our houseboy, who sets down a cup of tea on the coconut matting beside me. Abed is a charming rogue with a brilliant smile, and a white cap set on black curls. The brown boots are a present from Maurice and he wears them all the time, although they must hurt his bare feet terribly.

Everything we need is made locally. Today a group of girls came running down the road with freshly-sewn sheets, waving them above their heads like banners. Presents pour in – hares, pheasants, two live turkeys, firewood and a twenty-foot Christmas tree.

Our neighbour is a huge but kindly Kurd called Baban, who gets drunk and shoots off his gun at night. He has a pretty little French wife called Fifine who loathes Baghdad and longs for Paris. They arrived bearing roses, lemons and a very smelly wild duck, which Baban had shot.

To my great delight Rosemary Boxer, Mark Boxer's sister,

has come to live with us. She is a big, hearty girl, very jolly and friendly, and quite the opposite of Mark. She teaches English at the same college as Maurice.

The little hut at the bottom of our garden houses Abed's mother, Oom Abed, an old Bedouin witch in black, with silver anklets and a blue tattooed beard. Today she made me some extremely nasty flat bread on her charcoal brazier, while screeching and cursing at Abed who had stolen one of her anklets to go gambling.

Friday, 12 October. Clare's nanny has arrived – a seventeen-year-old Syrian Christian called Hanni. She is very well dressed and pretty and thinks all Arabs are dirty. Today she took away all my beautiful copper pots and trays and had them covered in tin, because she says copper is poisonous – I am furious!

Rosemary, who is an arty sort of girl, is helping me to do up the house with coconut matting and palm fronds and brightly coloured hangings woven by the Marsh people. Today in the bazaar she saw a huge ceramic pot which had been used to hold up a stall. She insisted on buying it and the poor man had to dismantle his whole stall. She is a very determined lady! Desmond – who can be a bitchy old queen at times – doesn't think much of our decor. 'Why have you done up your house like a second-rate mosque?' he demands scornfully.

Thursday, 1 November. After weeks of living on boiled eggs, we now have a cook! Hanni has imported her friend Youell, a servile and obsequious Armenian Christian with a wall eye. He is a disaster! We came home for dinner on his first night hoping for something spicy and oriental, and were greeted by a beaming Youell. 'Nice English food the way you like it!' he announced. 'Nice lamb chops, nice cauliflower in flour sauce!'

Monday, 5 November. Sacked Youell. Hired Machmoud, hoping he might prove a bit more ethnic: but not a hope – Abed had got in before us. He greeted us looking smug and triumphant in a brand new Dish-Dasha. 'Dinner very nice, sahib! I tell Machmoud you English no like Arabi food! I tell him no garlic, no spices, no rice! Look sahib, nice boiled carrots, nice chipped potatoes!' The carrots stood in a pool of tepid water, the chips were hard, and there were just a few lumps of gristly mutton in curried fat – Machmoud's only salute to the Orient.

Wednesday, 7 November. Sacked Machmoud and hired Abdul, a villainous Turk. Now indeed is the bitter bit, for Abdul not only cooks Arabic food – endless kibbehs and stuffed vegetables – but also makes enough for his wife and six children, which he takes home at night. He squats all day on the filthy kitchen floor moulding the rice stuffing in his sweaty palms. His voice is like a buzz-saw, and the sound of his constant sighing and complaining rings through the house. Every evening he demands money to buy soap and take a taxi to the *hammam* – the city's public baths.

Monday, 12 November. Sacked Abdul, who departed with two kilos of rice and one of our carpets under his arm. We have also sacked the cleaner, an endearing but ultimately useless fellow who wandered around the house very slowly, flicking at dust-motes with a palm frond.

So now the delighted Abed rules the roost. He adores Clare and is always stealing things for her – kittens, bunches of dates, and flowers from the public gardens. He and his mother carry her shoulder-high all over the house crowned with marigolds, and call her 'my heart and my two eyes'. Abed's idea of work is to sit on the verandah with his boots up and a flower behind his ear, reading Clare's fairy books upside down.

Rosemary and I have taken over the cooking. We use a biscuit tin for an oven and a tobacco tin as a measuring jug, and we are slowly working our way through Constance Spry – though without any conspicuous success, as most of her ingredients are unobtainable here. But we do have wonderful spices and also date syrup, pomegranate juice and a thick red tomato paste called *ma'jun*, which is dried out on the flat roofs of houses. Anything fresh and green has to be soaked in permanganate, as the irrigation ditches are hopping with nasty parasites. Hanni looks on disapprovingly. She knows only one dish – hard-boiled eggs encased in sausage meat, which she learnt from a previous employer – and is still waiting for a chance to make it.

Monday, 10 December. Rosemary is in love! He is a wonderful young doctor called Khalid Naji who is a communist and an atheist and treats the poor for free. He is very dynamic and sexy, and moves and speaks like a good animal that is happy inside its skin. I have rather a crush on him myself!

Saturday, 15 December. Khalid has taken over our lives, with interesting results. He pops in almost every evening with his little black bag full of strange substances for us to try. Last night it was opium, which made us very sleepy and sick! He and Rosemary are obviously having an affair, but have to be secretive about it on account of *aibh*. This word, which means shame, is one of the most powerful forces in the Arabic world, a word pronounced with dread and horror. It is because of *aibh* that poor Rosemary has to climb out of her window at night, bribe the guard who patrols the Waziriyah, ford a ditch, and climb a wall to get to his house. She gets home for breakfast in a dreadful state of disarray. There is something in the air here which makes you feel very sexy, very much a woman – something to do with the direct, hawk-like way the men look at you, I think!

Xmas Night 1951. An enormous party at Desmond's house with real turkey and Christmas pudding. We ate it to the accompaniment of three musicians playing strange instruments called oudhs and dimbuks, and a singer whose laments seemed half Negro, half flamenco. The Arab guests, seated on the floor in the firelight, groaned and cried out between each verse as if a finger had been drawn down their spines.

Meanwhile our neighbour Baban was shooting off his gun on the balcony, as is his wont when drunk, and his wife Fifine cornered me for a good moan. 'Je déteste Baghdad! Je suis interrée vive!' Apparently all her husband thinks about are his guns and 'la chasse' – he is a 'grand chasseur' and can pick up a jackel by its ears at full gallop. I escaped, and found two wonderful dancers with the unfortunate names of Morfuck and Mudhut. Mudhut is Baghdad's greatest exponent of the Viennese waltz. I kicked off my shoes and floated away in his arms. Rosemary played with Khalid's beads, the dreaded Mrs Prendergast did a Spanish castanet dance, and Desmond did a burlesque tango with his boyfriend. We all got terribly tiddly.

Wednesday, 2 January 1952. Tea with Khalid's three sisters, where I discover to my amazement that they have never seen the outside of their own front door. They will be in purdah until the day they marry – beautiful girls in silk dressing-gowns, who seem very happy surrounded by monkeys and parrots.

Eating sticky cakes around a simmering golden samovar, I asked them what they did with themselves all day. They replied that they, and their girlfriends who were not in purdah, led a most exhausting social life – 'We laugh, we cry, we tell tales, we play in the garden, we ride bicycles, we fall off – we laugh, we cry!' They share nothing with their menfolk, not even their meals, but in some ways are quite sophisticated. I was wearing my best dangly earrings from the bazaar but they were not impressed. 'Why do you wear those dreadful cheap earrings?' they asked. 'Only whores and gypsies wear such earrings! Why do you not wear diamonds?' I replied that I could not afford them, but they pretended not to hear, as this reflected the most terrible *aibh* on me.

After tea I went to visit Khalid's surgery, where he treats the poor of Baghdad for free – a really horrifying experience which I could hardly bear to watch. Half the men were suffering from stab wounds and broken heads, but there were also wretched women with ulcerous breasts and babies with rickets. Khalid was examining a woman who had some problem with her womb when her mother burst in screaming and shouting and dragged her out of the surgery. Apparently because the operation might mean she could bear no more sons, it was forbidden, so she will probably die in childbirth.

Maurice's students at the college are much more emancipated. They arrive shrouded in black abbas which they throw off to reveal tight-fitting skirts and sweaters with 'Wisconsin' printed on them. All the girls are in love with Mo because he is tall and blond. Unfortunately he has an awful habit of scratching his crotch when carried away by his own eloquence, and halfway through a lecture on Chaucer he'll notice fifty pairs of beady eyes glued to his trousers. Their work is excellent but erratic as they have a great desire to be colloquial – a splendid analysis of Hamlet's Act I will be followed by 'Well cheerio, so long, old sport – see you in Act II!'

Apart from the college teachers we avoid the English social scene as much as possible. The English Club is a walled-in ghetto where they eat roast pork under pictures of the royal family and have a Scottish dancing night on Fridays.

Monday, 21 January. Abed warns me that Hanni is going to take Clare to the public hangings! I stopped her just in time and tore her off a colossal strip!

Sunday, 27 January. Anniversary of the Portsmouth Treaty. The government has refused to let the students march to the cemetery and they are rioting in the college opposite where Maurice teaches. Police are firing and using tear gas, so I've sent Baban to extricate him. Baban roared off in his Cadillac with a couple of guns in the back and rescued Mo through a side door.

My only contact with the students is through thés dansants – they're all mad about dancing, and give little gramophone parties with tea and cakes where we foxtrot and samba. The boys are all very frustrated because they dare not touch any decent girl for fear of her family. They see Rosemary and me as manna from heaven and make heavy advances. One boy in particular, Khatan, pursues me relentlessly. He has a weird face like an Easter Island god, disfigured by Baghdad Boil pock-marks – rather attractive actually!

Tuesday, 29 January. Rosemary and I rashly agreed to go to a birthday party given by the lecherous Khatan. Everyone sat around the charcoal brazier smoking hash and making existentialist remarks such as 'il n'y a qu'une vie, il faut la vivre!' and so on. K. asked me where I got my drugs from and seemed rather surprised that I didn't have any. Everyone was wearing black and playing French songs on the gramophone. Later we jitterbugged madly and K. was murmuring 'Mrs Rowdon is marvellous!' He has christened me Cynara and Rosemary is Antigone. Got terribly drunk. At one in the morning he stopped his car outside our house and kissed me passionately and tried to persuade me to become his mistress. Unfortunately Mo was waiting up for me under the palm tree. He leapt out, dragged me from the car and beat me up in the garden. I got a black eye and lost one of my earrings. Hanni is most impressed by my shiner, I think she considers it a badge of honour on a good wife. Rosemary is still behaving badly too, staggering into breakfast covered in mud, sneaking into mosques dressed as an Arab, and getting arrested in the hospital, where she went to track down Khalid.

Thursday, 31 January. Beautiful spring weather, cold, dry and sunny. Our house is almost in the desert and we can see lines of camels from our bedroom window. I got up early and walked barefoot in the dewy grass looking for parsley and mint for my tabouleh salad. Unfortunately the best and greenest are growing round the sewer! Desmond came to lunch and we ate it on the roof with cool, creamy buffalo milk yoghurt set overnight in clay bowls. We bitch and gossip about the English community, the goings-on at the French embassy and who is Mrs Prendergast's latest lover. Desmond calls himself Snake and I am Lady Sneerwell. He is taking us to the races tomorrow.

Friday, 1 February. Our most exciting day yet. We were at the El Mansur race course by 7 a.m. to watch the trials from Colonel 'Dickie' Bird's flat inside the grandstand. We ate an enormous English breakfast of Cooper's Oxford marmalade and boiled eggs, and listened to records of 'Kiss Me, Kate'. Outside in the soft morning mist hundreds of horses in bright saddle-cloths were waiting for the gallops.

'The person we must find is Madame Paris,' Desmond said later as he shepherded us towards the betting hall: 'all the jockeys slept last night at her brothel and she knows which horses are being pulled or doped!'

Outside the paddock little Arab horses with hennaed fore-feet were ambling around in a circle to loud Arab music, some looking full of beans, others obviously doped to the eyebrows. We soon spotted Madame Paris, a short, fat woman with hennaed hair and puffy white cheeks, her mouth a red gash. She was shovelling money through the hatch with scarlet claws covered in rings. Desmond waylaid her and she whispered something in his ear. He came back beaming. 'Don't bet the favourite on the first race!' he announced. 'Madame P. says Mustapha is going to pull the horse!' Mustapha is one of the older jockeys, a great frequenter of Madame P.'s brothel and a drug addict. He is riding a horse belonging to Tariq, a senior government official's son, who doesn't want it to win – he is betting heavily on the second favourite.

It was time for the first race. All around the course hundreds of Arabs in sheepskin coats crouched on benches like huge birds, their grey pin-striped skirts drawn up between their bare legs.

There was a wild cry of 'Zerroff!' and the little horses disappeared in a cloud of dust, the jockeys hanging on to the britches of the one in front – except of course for the ones who had been paid to lose, and they were pulling on the reins like mad. Inexplicably Mustapha seemed to be winning. Wild with delight the crowded benches leapt in the air with cries of 'Hamdillillah!' – 'Praise be to Allah!' 'Oh dear,' said Desmond, 'poor Mustapha *will* be in trouble! He wasn't pulling nearly hard enough, and Tariq will have lost a packet.'

Sure enough, just as we were about to go, there was a wild outcry from the bar, where Tariq was drowning his sorrows in drink. He had struck Mustapha and Mustapha had struck him back. As two soldiers dragged the jockey from the grand-stand and manhandled him through the crowds, he shouted obscenities against the government, reserving his choicest language for Tariq, a well-known queer. 'OH FATHER OF PRICKS,' he yelled, 'so many times has thine arse been breeched that . . .' The rest is so awful that I really can't write it! The crowd listened in deep and delighted silence.

That very night Mustapha was helped to escape by the Regent, whose lover he is, and has gone into the desert to join the tribes. Madame Paris can now dine out on it for weeks – 'Mustapha he say!' – cackle cackle.

'Not much like good old Epsom, is it, dear?' Desmond said as we drove back in his car. 'No,' I said, 'but much more fun!'

Thursday, 13 March. Picnic at Babylon. It is almost perfectly preserved, and you can walk along its streets. We spread a carpet beside the walls and smoked hashish under a cloudless sky while an old man played us haunting music on a rebaba. In the evening we went to see a dreadful Jayne Mansfield film of which only about a quarter was visible owing to three lots of ethnic sub-titles and bicycles parked along the screen. This didn't stop the audience from fighting to get seats in the gallery so they could get a better view of Jayne Mansfield in the bath!

Saturday, 1 March. A typical domestic day. In the morning a box arrived from the 'dairy fagtory' labelled 'beast butter'. Despatched Abed to the market to get us a chicken while we went to Mackinnon's store, a haven of English goodies. We returned laden with Tiptree jams, Marmite and digestive biscuits to find Abed brandishing a bloody axe and a headless chicken racing around and round the garden, just as you'd always heard they did but never quite believed it.

Abed then announced that the drains were blocked – a common occurrence – but that he had sent for the Father of Lavatories, who shortly after arrives on his bicycle hung around with suction tubes.

After dinner, Mo's tailor turned up bearing a terrible ape-man linen suit with huge shoulders. There is also a rabbit in our *hammam*.

Tuesday, 18 March. Our Kurdish neighbour Baban is showing alarming signs of infatuation. Last night he took us to the gypsies who are camped on the outskirts of the city. We watched them dance – rather badly – in their dusty velvet hung with coins, while Baban's sinister chauffeur had a great time with one of their sisters in the tent next door.

While we were driving back, B., who was drunk, announced solemnly, 'I *loove* Mrs Rowdon!' The chauffeur gave a violent

twitch and his ears pricked up so much that his cap practically
shot off his head. He is Fifine's ally and confidante, and sure
enough a Patchouli-scented note, written in green ink, arrived
next day by the hand of a servant. It was brief and to the
point. 'Voulez vous cesser de vous accrocher a mon mari et
de metre la discorde dans notre marriage. On dit que les
Anglais sont des gens correctes!' It was signed Fifine B.

Baban, who is very fond of Maurice, was deeply upset, and
went straight to the market place in search of a scribe. 'Dear
Brother,' the scribe wrote for him, 'I don't know really how
I should approach you to beg you to be so kind as to forgive
me for the incident that took place yesterday and to the
objectionable behaviour expressed by me while not under my
control! My wife is much aroused by jealousy, but women
after all are women! You must believe, dear Brother, that I
always looked upon Mrs Rowdon with due respect and as a
sister.' Well of course we all made friends again, but Fifine
no longer asks us to lunch.

Tuesday, 1 April. Today the heat began. The eucalyptus trees
along the street are shrouded in dust and the whole Waziriyah
smells of orange blossom. I am bored and restless. I was out
walking in the sun-baked town when I heard wailing and
drums and suddenly, from round the corner, a funeral burst
upon me – women with whitened faces ululating like furies,
tearing their clothes and beating their breasts, a nightmare in
broad daylight.

To alleviate my boredom I have taken a job teaching
English to a Jewish girl called Vivvi Solomon, who is fat and
rather stupid. Her rich parents live in a house stuffed with
tasteless furniture, but they pay me very well – £2 a session –
and ply me with sticky cakes and coffee. Unfortunately my
efforts to interest Vivvi in *Tess of the D'Urbevilles* have fallen
on deaf ears as all she wants to talk about is social life in
London and whether I think she could join The Monkey
Club and be a debutante. What does one wear when presented
at Court? What did I think of Mrs Simpson? What sort of
dresses do they wear at the 400 Club? As my own knowledge
of smart society is nil, our afternoons pass slowly.

Clare, on the other hand, is happy as a sandboy and has
gone completely native! She speaks perfect gutter Arabic and

has a host of filthy little friends who live in the garden next door with a gazelle and a long-eared woolly sheep. Her special friend is Affra, as black as Clare is blonde, with a face like Nefertiti and a little blue tattooed beard. Enemy children are sent off by Clare who stands on the doorstep screaming 'Imshi y'allah, ibn el kelb' which roughly means 'Buzz off, son-of-a-dog!' From my bedroom window I can see them darting through the Waziriyah like a flock of birds, occasionally swooping down with lifted skirts to pee in the gutter.

Saturday, 5 April. Crisis with Hanni – nearly lost her. She had dragged Clare away from her little friends muttering 'Dirty, dirty!' and had taken her to the *hammam* to wash her hair against lice. When the soap got in Clare's eyes it was the last straw. Wriggling free she screamed 'Akkli khara bint et gawad' which means 'Eat shit, thou daughter of a pimp!' Hanni finally agreed to stay, but we had to raise her wages.

Thursday, 10 April. Rosemary has had a terrible accident. She and I were out riding beyond the racecourse on big unmanageable horses when Rosemary's horse bolted and threw her on stony ground. Waiting for help was terrifying – R. was frothing at the mouth and having fits, her eyes crossed and her legs kicking spasmodically. She was rushed to the hospital and I went in search of Khalid, who was doing his rounds in another ward. When I told him that Rosemary had been thrown, his hand tightened uncontrollably on his worry beads, the string split and a cascade of amber rattled over the shiny wooden floor, startling the sick peoples' relatives who were crouched by the beds over their cooking pots. Now I knew that Khalid really loved her.

Thank God it's only concussion, nothing fatal. It means she will miss our trip to Kurdistan next week. Baban is going there to plot and to visit his relatives, and he is taking us with him. His blind cousin Ali, who lives at Kifri, is a leading figure in the fight for Kurdish independence.

Tuesday, 5 April. We set off for Kasarabad in his enormous car, Baban driving like a maniac with much shouting of 'Son-of-a-dog!' to competing motorists.

His relatives live in a dusty walled compound. They are fierce and beautiful with blue-grey eyes, hung around with rifles and cartridge belts, their turbans rakishly tied.

Clare was despatched on a donkey ride, disappearing in a cloud of dust in the grip of a most villainous-looking character. I was banished to the harem to drink sweet tea and eat cakes with a gaggle of gold-toothed wives who insisted on dressing me up in Kurdish clothes. Sweating away in layers of velvet and flowery prints, with a rather fetching head-dress fringed with coins, I finally got up enough courage to ask for the lavatory. A servant led me behind a hut and pointed to a hole in the ground. I peered nervously into it and saw with alarm the sparkling eyes and pointed whiskery snout of a large rat.

Meanwhile Mo was also being decked out in Kurdish gear complete with turban, rifle and a very bad-tempered hawk on his wrist. I don't know who looked more nervous, Mo or the hawk.

After dinner I had a game of poker with three fierce-looking cousins who played with their rifles propped up against their chairs. I lost heavily, being far too frightened to bluff.

We slept in a huge bed with a lattice-work ceiling. At dawn the wooden rafters stirred with life and myriads of birds left their nests to shit on our heads and swoop out of the window.

Friday, 11 April. We drove by the ruined castle of a robber baron to Kifri, home of the blind rebel Ali. He and Baban went inside to plot and I sat in the sun looking down to the dried-up river where a poor bear had been tied to a post. Watching it dance round in frantic circles, teased and tortured by Ali's servants, I became more and more depressed and enraged. Later, when Ali offered to give me a piece of silk, which I had rashly admired, I took my courage in both hands. 'Thank you, no, but there is something which I would like very much better.' Everybody looked shocked, especially Baban, as I had obviously made a terrible faux pas. 'It's the bear,' I persisted. 'I would be very happy if you would set it free.' Ali seemed to think I was mad. 'The bear is far from its home – it will never get back to the hills before somebody shoots it.' 'Yes, but it will die free.' I'd obviously struck the right note, for Ali's face changed. 'That I can understand – we have a saying in my country, Kurdistan ya namash, Kurdistan or death. I swear by my eyes, the bear shall have its chance.' He clapped his hands and a sulky-looking servant went to relay the bad news to the bear's tormentors.

A few minutes later I saw the lumbering creature, still bemused and uncertain of his direction, loping off across the dry river bed and vanishing into the dusty hills beyond.

Friday, 17 April. To the Black Place, where we rode on little fast horses with flat stirrups as big as plates through fields of wild tulips. Our guide pointed to the mountains on the horizon and said 'Persia!'

Over a very tough, newly-killed chicken, our host told me that I was a better rider than my husband – Mo was not at all pleased at that! In the afternoon we visited the souk where the men bought coloured bridles for themselves, and pink plastic cartridge-belts and gun holsters for their children. At night everyone got drunk and stood on the balcony firing off their rifles, so I fled to my room, fingers in ears.

Glad to get back to Baghdad, to clean lavatories and own cooking.

Rosemary is back from hospital, a little shaky and forgetful but okay. Khalid visits her every day.

Thursday, 1 May. Time is running out – soon the heat will be so great that Clare and I will have to go back to London, so I am accepting all and any invitations that come my way, even from the dreaded English community. Imagine my delight then to be invited to a party given by a real sheikh, a breed I have not yet encountered.

The sheikh and his four brothers greeted us on the patio of their immense modern house. They were all over six foot and draped in magnificent cloaks. Inside there was practically no furniture – just an enormous refrigerator, some hubble-bubbles and a few rickety-looking chairs and sofas in the 'Empire' style made out of orange boxes, the fronts richly brocaded, the backs made from cheap wood with 'Basra' stamped on it.

The guests sat solemnly ranged around the walls while a

gypsy band squatted in the centre of the floor playing on drums and violins made out of old Castrol tins. The gypsy chief was a magnificent figure, his mouth open in a permanent gap-toothed leer, his turban cocked over one eye. He sang in a hoarse and impassioned voice to the music of his Castrol tin. There was, of course, the usual bad gypsy dancer in dusty velvet.

The sheikhs lolled on gilded sofas with an air of sophisticated boredom, quizzing the dancers with their arrogant eyes and playing with their huge amber beads. They were flanked by gypsy girls who giggled and toyed with their hair (the sheikhs' hair, that is). Behind them glowered their bodyguards, bristling with knives and guns, and peering between the guards' legs – puce with excitement – were the children of the house. The windows were blacked-out by the grimy, grinning faces of the tribesmen, climbing on each other's shoulders to view the show.

I was getting hungry and I could see the dinner – two roasted sheep – getting extremely cold on the verandah. We ate about midnight, squatting on the floor. Sheep delicious (no eyeballs, thank God) but also various stews of what looked like innards, rather daunting.

While tearing at the sheep I couldn't help thinking of the poor mud hut villages that Khalid had taken us to, where rice is a treat eaten once a year on feast days. 'We eat grass, the sheikhs are starving us!' they had told us.

Our last few days were spent almost entirely with Khalid, whom we loved. One night he told us he had a great treat for us – his little half-Negro assistant was getting married, and we were invited to the *male* party. The bride of course, has her own women's do, but apparently, being English, Rosemary and I are considered sexless!

It was held in an old Turkish house in the slums, with smoke-blackened rooms set around a central courtyard. By the light of a storm lantern we could see fifty odd men in an ecstatic state of intoxication singing to a band of dimbuks, rebabas and tambourines, squatting on the floor and swaying in a rhythmic trance, their turbans tied in fantastic shapes in honour of the wedding.

For us – the honoured guests – there was a battered settee set on a raised platform and a little table laid with everything they imagined that the English liked – Haig whisky, bully-beef, tinned herrings in tomato sauce, Kraft cheese and Craven A cigarettes. It was somehow immensely touching. Beside us sat Khalid, lounging back in a graceful, arrogant way and playing with his beads, while a student sang us a song of welcome.

Suddenly the crowd began to ululate like wolves and the wretched bridegroom, who had returned from the mosque, was dragged in, looking pale and apprehensive. He kissed our hands and sat beside us on the settee, calling for the dancing girl, a beautiful creature accompanied by her 'manager'. She had long hennaed hair to her waist, barbaric jewellery and wore a fur stole over a white lace garden-party dress. 'It is, of course, a man!' Khalid whispered in my ear, much to my amazement. Apparently they are hermaphrodites known as Sha'ah, meaning 'hair', trained from childhood in a male brothel. His make-up and false bosoms were pretty convincing, though rather let down by several flashing gold teeth and a heavy man's wristwatch. His dancing, which was a cross between Spanish and Negro, involved much hip-shaking, clacking of castanets and shaking out his mane of hair like a banner. Strangely enough it was most seductive and very beautiful.

I had an urgent need to pee and was ushered into the garden where there was a sinister-looking hut on stilts. Climbing up, I peered inside. The moon shone through a hole in the roof onto a quite staggering pyramid of turds. I decided to risk the bushes, and was still crouching when the guests suddenly erupted into the garden, led by the dancer who was waving a red veil to simulate virgin blood. The men fell on the ground shuddering and moaning in a kind of orgasmic trance, while the dancer swept her raised skirts and her veil over them. This was obviously no time to get caught with one's knickers down, so I quickly made myself decent and emerged nonchalantly from the oleanders, just in time to see the unfortunate bride-groom carried off shoulder-high to his waiting bride, followed closely by his mother-in-law whose job it was to seize the bloodied sheets and hang them out of the window.

* * *

Monday, 5 May. I am dreading going back to London – and I wonder how Clare will feel? I know she is only three, but she's so happy and well-adjusted here. This morning I looked down from the balcony outside my bedroom and saw her dancing alone in the early morning sunlight with a towel wrapped round her waist. She wore little bells on her ankles and was doing a childish parody of a belly-dancer – a step to the right, a step to the left and then a shaking of her non-existent hips. In the evening Hanni carried her off to say goodbye to her family in the slums, and I watched her vanishing like a white moth into the darkness.

We sat up all night in a café with Khalid, Desmond, Alan, Maurice and Rosemary and ate kebab and got drunk from a hip-flask. Khalid talked of suicide. On the radio a famous singer called Oom Kathoom was singing 'The Rubaiyat of Omar Khyam'. Then Khalid sang for us, a song about a man who loves both his friend and his lover – 'Oh night, Oh eyes!' We hear this refrain often in the city – many singers set the mood for their songs with it and we hear it in cars, on the radio, and in cafés. It is the very sound of Baghdad.

Khalid gave me his beads and a little bag of *Numi basrah*, the dried lemons with the haunting scent that we use to perfume our tea.

I am catching the Nairn desert bus to Beirut tomorrow – I can't believe I am really going.

Chapter Four

Clare and I arrived on the doorstep of No. 5 Redcliffe Gardens, only to find that I'd forgotten my keys. I rang the doorbell, hoping that Shura, my lodger, would be in. How nice it would be, I thought, to spend a couple of months with him and his lovely girlfriend. Shura opened the door and seemed delighted to see me, but told me rather sadly that Bianca had gone back to New York to see her parents. In the pause that followed I felt all my nerve ends tingling. There was an amazing electricity between us, a premonition of exciting and upsetting things to come. The two Jamaicans and the second-hand car dealers had both left, so we had the house to ourselves.

In the weeks that followed we became more and more fond of each other, doing all the things that courting couples do without actually touching each other. We picnicked in Kew Gardens, visited the Zoo, and rowed on the Serpentine. Shura cooked wonderful Russian and Chinese meals, played gypsy music on my mother's ukulele and introduced me to his friends from university who held wild poker parties two or three times a week.

We were of course different in every way – I am English and Catholic, he is of Russian extraction, brought up in China – but this was what particularly appealed to me. After the aridity of my own family life it was wonderful to be with someone who had been brought up by a warm, loving, closely-knit family, and still kept in touch with relatives all over the world. Although we had not yet made love, I was completely happy and relaxed with him, with a feeling of expectancy, as if it was always Christmas morning. It was that thrilling period when two people know in their bones that something is going to happen, but want to prolong the waiting.

Then one night came the crunch. I went to have a bath and while I was out of the room Shura threw on a dressing-gown of black Chinese silk, lit six candles and an incense stick and laid out two glasses and a bottle of vodka on the ironing board. Then he seized the ukulele and flung himself on my bed. It was irresistible!

There is no painless way to end a marriage, and mine was no exception. Nearly two years of misery and deception followed, with guilty afternoon visits to Shura's digs in Notting Hill. Then, to make matters worse, I discovered I was pregnant. I toyed with the idea of an abortion but found myself unable to go through with it.

When my daughter Camilla was finally born, the hollow shell of our marriage finally cracked. Maurice, who had been muttering about blood-tests, took one look at this minuscule replica of my lover and agreed to a separation. He moved to Rome with a new girlfriend, and Clare, Camilla and I stayed on in Redcliffe Gardens.

Although Shura was by then working in Fleet Street, we were still pretty skint, but then came an amazing stroke of luck. Lord Glenconnor, Colin Tennant's father – who was some sort of a vague 'cousin' – decided to take a fatherly interest in me. (He also admired my shoulders, which I had taken the opportunity of displaying in a topless sheath dress one night at the Milroy.) He offered to fund any small business I liked to start, provided it was profitable for both of us, and as espresso bars were all the rage at that moment I decided to open the first one in Oxford.

I found a ramshackle old premises over a hat shop in the Cornmarket, and enlisted the help of a brilliant young Italian architect called Germano Facetti. Together we gutted it, and gave it the full Fifties coffee-bar treatment – Formica tables, spindly metal chairs, mosaic murals, hundreds of pot plants and everything painted brilliant red, black and white. In one corner was an enormous hissing Gaggia machine which bore the unlikely legend 'It works without steam'. We also invested in a load of Lucy Rie ashtrays – cheap in those days, now collectors' items – and a pile of the grooviest records we could find, starting off with 'Rock Around the Clock' and Presley's 'Heartbreak Hotel'. I recruited a gang of friends to work with me and we moved into the two top floors, a honeycomb of tiny rooms with cardboard partitions – 'Just like a Roman brothel', as one of my friends remarked.

Saturday, 28 January 1956. Opening day. By six o'clock the sign over the door was still not finished, and the signwriter – spurred on by endless glasses of wine – was getting drunker and drunker. By the time he finished, with only half an hour to spare, the last A of ROMA was practically trailing off the bottom of the board.

Half the students in Oxford – agog to see their new watering-hole – turned up for the party and were later seen staggering down the Cornmarket laden with our best Lucy Rie ashtrays and a huge eucalyptus plant in a pot like Huns leaving a sacked city. Later, at a party given by some students in our honour, we thought the music sounded familiar – and sure enough, there were our precious records stacked up by the gramophone. My faith in the probity of Oxford undergraduates had received its first blow.

Next day I woke up at 6 a.m., took three Alka-Seltzers and stumbled down to the kitchen. Here I was confronted by a bloody mound of raw chopped beef, and another of mince, which were to be converted by twelve o'clock into goulash and spaghetti bolognaise. I had never cooked for more than six people in my life and the sight of all that meat, not to mention the gargantuan saucepans and huge gas range, absolutely terrified me.

I was in floods of tears when a little man with a black beard called Gustavus arrived on a motorbike to fix the gramophone. He positively fizzed with energy like a tiny firecracker, and when I heard that he had worked in restaurants I roped him in to help without further delay. In no time at all he had the bolognaise sauce and the goulash on the go, and the spaghetti on the boil. While it was cooking he would occasionally pick out a few strands and hurl them at the wall – if they slithered down they were done, if they stuck they needed a few more minutes. Being of Dutch-German extraction, he also had a great vocabulary of German oaths.

I soon learnt to do six things at once, sweating and swearing like a trooper, and by the time the hatch shot up and the first waitress jammed her chit on the spike with a yell of 'One spag bol!' I was ready for action.

Meanwhile downstairs, Oxford's most glamorous waitresses were whirling between the Formica tables, their huge six-tiered starched petticoats knocking the froth from the cappuccinos. One of them was heiress Sarah Rothschild, who was in love with the barman; the others were two gorgeous Jamaican sisters, Daphne and Lola, and the daughter of the Pakistani ambassador. John Constable, a descendant of the painter, was behind the Gaggia.

I was having a rest and an espresso when Val, my ultra-cool manager, came up. 'I don't want to alarm you, but there is a very Zen citizen doing the washing-up!' I peered around the corner of the bar and saw a turbaned Sikh pouring yet another bottle of detergent into what looked like a bubble bath. As he rolled his purple-veined eyes towards me I noticed that he was smoking two cigarettes simultaneously, one sticking out of each side of his mouth like a cat's whiskers. He turned out to be on parole from the local mental home where they seemed to think this sort of work would do him good.

We had another barman called Peter who was studying Tibetan. He had the tiniest attic room of all, known as Little Hell, where he spent a lot of his spare time standing on his head. Val said he was deeply into the phases of the moon and could only make love when it was full, so we had to arrange his working hours accordingly.

*

Monday, 13 February. Two weeks on and I have now got the kitchen finally organised. Gus and I take turns to do the cooking and we have two kitchen helpers who, unfortunately, are both epileptic. One is a lovely old lady called Momma, who has left the marmalade factory to work for us, and there is Keith, a tall lad with a broken nose, the result of falling so often into the cooking pans. Since his last encounter with the hot plate he has started wearing a crash helmet. We keep a mattress under the kitchen table in case Momma has a turn and I always have a wooden spoon handy in my apron pocket to stop them swallowing their tongues.

The students love the place, and use it as their club, chatting up the waitresses and bringing their favourite records for us to play, while they sit for hours over one cappuccino. Some of the out-of-college ones, who don't like their digs, more or less live in the warm and cosy kitchen. They roost like chickens among the potato sacks, their noses buried in Nietzsche and Wittgenstein. Socially, their attitude towards us is ambivalent. We occasionally get asked to college parties, but on the whole we are viewed as some strange and exotic gypsy encampment that has set up its alien tents among the dreaming spires. At night the mescalin boys arrive, young rakes from the science lab with squash bottles full of home-brewed hallucinogens sticking out of their duffle-coat pockets – some of them even bring their own straws. 'Scheis!' mutters Gus, 'here comes the cactus juice brigade!' They wander round the kitchen in search of interesting scents and colours. Apparently La Roma and the Ashmolean Museum are considered by connoisseurs to be the best places in Oxford to hallucinate in.

Our cooking is fairly basic. The cooked spaghetti is stored in a huge dustbin, and from there transferred to a steam cabinet where it is kept in a hot state, far from *al dente*. On the stove there are two simmering pots of spag sauce (bol and nap) and a saucepan of goulash. We also do savoury pancakes, omelettes and knackwurst with sauerkraut. Owing to the persistent demand for chips we have finally given in and screwed a big, brutish hand chipper to the edge of the wooden table. These are fried up in batches, using a saucepan of hot oil and a wire strainer.

Downstairs things are more elegant, with open sandwiches and Danish pastries, in the style of the famous El Cubano in Knightsbridge.

Every night there is music – jazz or skiffle – with Bernard Cash on trumpet, Ogden on guitar and Gus beating the hell out of a washboard. The whole house vibrates to 'Cumberland Gap', 'Six-Five Special', 'T for Texas' and 'The Foggy Foggy Dew'.

Soon after midnight, when the café is closed, the silence is broken by the trampling of heavy feet and a slow, mournful rendition of 'The Volga Boat Song' as our two queer kitchen porters – both resting 'actors' – stagger downstairs with the reeking dustbins. Rob is butch and Dennis is weedy, but he has lately been going in for body-building and announced proudly last week that he is thinking of 'turning into a man'. We hear extraordinary sounds coming from his room upstairs as he practises his new manly voice – lots of 'yo heave ho's', followed by snatches of Pagliacci. He definitely thinks he can see more hairs growing on his chest.

I have taken a flat with a garden in Woodstock Road for the children and their Spanish au pair, Maria Dolores. She is a small bossy little number with a red Eton crop who likes to deck the children's hair with daisy chains, put on their smartest dresses and parade them up and down the High as if it was the Ramblas in Barcelona. As she seems to feed them almost entirely on Marmite sandwiches I make sure she brings them every day to the kitchen for a square meal. Shura is working in London as a freelance journalist, and only comes up for weekends, so I prefer to sleep in my tiny cubicle over the café where I can keep an eye on things. I love to lie there listening to the city's endlessly chiming clocks, feeling the whole café beneath me buzzing and vibrating with a life of its own. This must be one of the happiest periods of my life and I wish it would never end. We are of course, all desperately tired, working twelve-hour shifts, seven days a week. Sometimes we just stumble around bumping into each other like zombies, swearing horribly, shouting curses to relieve the unbearable stress. But there is this wonderful feeling of comradeship which I think you only get with people you work and suffer with, when all pretences have been wiped out.

* *

Tuesday, 1 May. A really bad day. The cat has crapped in the brown sugar sack again, and the Gaggia machine, for the umpteenth time, has leaked through the ceiling onto Muriel's Modes below, thus ruining a whole shopful of dreadful May Week hats. Momma has threatened, for the umpteenth time, to go back to the marmalade factory. Our delivery of knack-wurst was delivered in a very odd condition, with little patches of white mould on it. 'Scheis mit reis und gherkin salat!' screeched Gus, picking up a sausage and eyeing it distaste-fully. 'Have these bloody knacks got athlete's foot or some-thing?' He wanted to mince them up and bung them in the bol sauce but I wouldn't let him, so we had a row. Finally Dennis, after announcing that he has turned into a man, has bought himself a cloth cap and a knapsack and has gone off to be a railway porter. Poor Robbie is heartbroken.

Over the next few months I found myself far too busy and tired to keep a diary. Also we were worried stiff over money, or rather the lack of it. Our main problem was to get the students to pay – which was strictly against their principles, especially if they were being served by a girlfriend. Even on a *good* day, our till was £3 or £4 short, largely because the staff used it as their private bank. An extremely large compartment in it was always stuffed with IOUs – many of them from Boris, our resident professor, a venerable bearded figure in a black Homburg who drank endless lemon teas but never had any money.

Finally, in despair, I asked a friend of mine to take over as manager and help get the place on its feet. His first act was to relocate the till right by the exit, like a tank trap; it was manned by an enormous, moustachioed Irish lady in black. Shock, horror! What? *Pay* at La Roma? We also put up some of the prices and introduced a few high-class dishes like steak and chips. This did not go down at all well with the students. 'I come in for a quiet cappuccino,' complained one of our oldest customers, 'and what do I find? A till at the door, and a load of shit-house squares in fancy waistcoats noshing the old fillet steak at 5/6d a go! *Where are your principles?*'

* * *

Sunday, 11 November. There has been an uprising in Hungary against the Communist regime, and the students here are in a state of great excitement. Some of the more fiery and romantic ones have even gone out to join in the fighting, and some of our friends have actually been put in prison.

Those who have returned sit in the café wearing fur hats and looking smug and heroic, which more or less guarantees them free coffees from admiring waitresses.

Friday, 17 December. We are still immensely popular, but slowly the dreadful truth is beginning to dawn on us – we are not making any money and will soon be broke. Christopher Glenconnor, who is first and foremost a shrewd businessman, thinks we should 'go professional', so I have found a young Italian called Raffaele who will run the place for us as a proper Italian trattoria. Our waitresses Daphne and Lola have hit on a great wheeze. We, in return, should go to Italy and open a string of 'infuso bars' serving strong tea. There will be a rain machine outside the window, kippers on the menu, Gracie Fields on the hi-fi and waitresses in cardigans and kirbygrips.

Thursday, 10 January 1957. Our last night. We had a skiffle group playing in the kitchen, and God knows how anyone got served. We flipped pancakes to 'Yellow Dog Blues', fried chips to 'Careless Love', stirred the goulash to 'St James's Infirmary'. We jived to the hatch and back again to the stove, beating out the rhythm as we went on saucepan lids, and by the end of the evening there wasn't a drop of cooking sherry left in the house.

Next day the red plus banquettes and the pepper-grinders moved in, and the fun was finally over.

Chapter Five

𝒩 Meanwhile, back at Redcliffe Gardens, dirty work was afoot. I had let the room underneath to a 'frightfully nice girl' called Fenella, who had taken advantage of our absence to improve her status in life.

Her first ploy had been to have an extension phone put in so she could make long-distance calls on my account. Then, finding her surroundings a bit too cramped for her liking, she took an electric saw to the partition wall and broke through into my storeroom, putting a large padlock on the outside door. Any attempts on our part to force the door and gain access resulted in instant writs for assault and battery. Her only worry was that, as the tenant of a furnished room, she could be booted out, so she decided to make herself secure by the simple expedient of throwing all my furniture out of the window to the rag-and-bone man below. Her final piece of bare-faced cheek was to take me to the Rent Tribunal and get her rent reduced to ten bob a week because I had not provided her with any furniture. (The law in those days was totally on the side of the tenant.)

I knew when I was beaten, and sold the whole flat with Fenella in it for £200 to a well-known man about Chelsea called Kim Caborn-Waterfield, who hinted darkly that he and his friends had means of dealing with slags like Fenella.

By now I had had enough of Redcliffe Gardens, and yearned for the King's Road, which, in the late Fifties, still felt like a genuine village, with a thriving artists' community, good local shops and atmospheric old pubs.

'You probably won't like this house,' the King's Road estate agent told us: 'it's an ugly, run-down sort of place, and the old chap who lives in it won't take a penny under £6,000!' He was referring to a beautiful Georgian five-storey house in Wellington Square off the King's Road – the sort of place that goes nowadays for well over half a million.

We got a mortgage and took it like a shot, even though it was in a terrible condition, divided up into lots of bedsitters, and done up throughout with treacly-brown scumbled wallpaper and fake panelling.

To add to my happiness, Maurice at long last decided to give me a divorce, so I could finally get married to Shura. This delighted my mother as now she could see me as a respectable woman, even if I was in mortal sin.

Cammy told a shocked headmistress that she was taking the day off to see her Daddy and Mummy get married, and there was a wild wedding party, with lots of Russian dancing and gypsy guitarists. About a hundred people turned up, and I danced all night in a pale blue dress which soon got splashed with red wine.

Around five in the morning my new husband drove off with his friend Jeremy Hadfield to another party in Hampstead. I woke up on my wedding morning, stretched out an affectionate arm towards the other side of the bed and encountered Jeremy's baby son in a carry-cot. Two hours later Shura and Jeremy returned, both roaring pissed, and demanded that I should cook them breakfast. My life as a Russian bride had begun.

We spent our honeymoon in the mountains of Macedonia, where we had heard there were some spectacular peasant weddings with gypsy music. We were searching for a village called Gari, which was just a dot on the map. Needless to say the bus stopped many miles short of it, and we had to continue our journey on mules, spurred on by the sound of distant drums. We were also encouraged by the sight of other wedding guests hurrying along, all in traditional peasant dress, with the exception of one smart lady in a turquoise two-piece, who spoiled the general effect by carrying her handbag on her head.

We reached Gari just as the wedding procession was winding down the village street on horseback, led by a band of gypsy musicians. A man with a wheatsheaf tied to his back, representing fertility, seized my hand so hard that my rings bit into the flesh, pressed a bottle of homemade slivowitz to my lips and dragged me into a dancing circle. The friendliness of these people and the hospitality shown us was quite amazing. There was one incident that I found particularly touching. I noticed a young girl kneeling at my feet, sewing up the hem of my skirt: she had noticed that it had fallen down and had run all the way back to her hut to fetch needle and thread.

The head man asked us in for a meal and offered us some extremely nasty-looking goat, cut from a haunch that hung in the rafters. 'Eat it if it kills you!' Shura hissed in my ear. 'You can't refuse Balkan hospitality!' Soon I felt griping pains and desperately wanted to go to the loo. As I looked around frantically the old grannie took me by the hand and led me to a deep ravine, with a rickety bridge spanning the foaming river below. In the middle of the bridge there was a hole, to which she pointed proudly. As I crouched nervously over the roaring torrent she politely turned her back on me and put her fingers in her ears. I spent a restless night sleeping over the bar, kept awake by indigestion from the goat and by the village policeman in the room below, who kept shooting his pistol at the ceiling.

Next day there were more gypsies, more dancing in the street and more homemade slivowitz – I was getting tired of surreptitiously wiping the mouth of the bottle on my skirt. Eventually we had a few days of rest and recuperation in Dubrovnik, swimming in clear green water that smelt like freshly-cut cucumbers. While there we were lucky enough to contact a lovely girl, Mira, who agreed to come to London as our au pair, replacing the Spanish girl, whom the children loathed. She turned out to be a great success, although she could only cook noodles and pancakes, and the children adored her.

My eldest daughter, Clare, was finding it difficult to accept her new Daddy. Lying comfortably in bed on a Sunday morning reading the newspapers, we would hear whispers and scuffling outside our door. Clare, armed with a fairy wand from the dressing-up chest, was about to conduct the brain-washed Camilla in an anti-Shura song. 'Mummy is our Mummy!' they carolled in unison: 'Granny is our Granny! Maurice is our Daddy! But' – *fortissimo* – 'SHURA'S JUST A FRIEND!' I managed to restrain S. from leaping out of bed and thumping them, and after a few months finally Clare accepted him.

My mother also took a great shine to Shura once she was finally convinced that he was not a dangerous Communist and asked us down to stay at the cottage in Wendover where she spent her summers. But not so her new companion, Rosamund. Shura made the mistake of saying 'Bugger!' in front of her when he stubbed his toe, and whenever we visited their cottage, she could be seen fleeing across the field with her suitcase.

Even so, I was extremely relieved that my mother had got someone to live with her, as she had been very lonely since Sid died. She told me how happy she was when she first saw Rosamund coming downstairs from her bedroom at the cottage and realised she was really going to stay for good, and how squiffy they got on sherry that night. Next day they picked bluebells in Wendover woods, and sent them off in damp collapsing cardboard boxes to a charity called the Loaves and Fishes, which aimed to brighten up the lives of distressed gentle folk.

Rosamund's deceptively mild and humble exterior concealed a will of steel. She and my mother occasionally had awful rows, and my mother once threw a camp bed at her. But when they were not rowing they led chaste and happy lives, drinking sherry, doing tapestry, playing their ukuleles and reading aloud to each other from the classics. Sometimes they watched television, but this was a bit tricky as R. was a fearful prude, and the slightest suggestion of sex sent her running to hide in the bathroom where she made a pretence of washing out her undies. Even well-vetted wildlife programmes were not safe, as they might feature a mating spider.

I adored my mother, and some of our happiest times were spent at the cottage – on old shepherd's hut in a field which she bought for a song after the War, and converted into a veritable paradise.

Over the next few years I had a variety of jobs. I worked as an A.S.M. at the Canonbury Theatre, and as a reader for James Michie at The Bodley Head. I even wrote wildly inaccurate horoscopes for *Honey* magazine. I finally ended up as the food writer for *What's On*, where all the restaurants, no matter how grotty, had to be praised because they were advertisers. One found ways around this, of course: 'A strange and unusual combination', for instance, meant horrible and uneatable. I read the contributions from previous writers and made certain resolutions: *never* would I 'browse' through the wine list, 'toy' with my spaghetti, 'plump joyfully' for the *riz de veau*, describe scallops as 'sparkling fresh' or the curry as 'tongue-tingling'. Never would my stomach sing hosannahs as I dived into the chocolate mousse, and under no circumstances would I refer to my 'companion of the evening' – hack-speak for lover getting a free meal.

However, I soon got tired of freelance work, and in 1958 I managed to land a job in Fleet Street, as assistant Home Editor on a glossy magazine called *Housewife*. I did the shopping pages for men and women – which was nice, because I got a lot of free samples and could pick all the dishiest male models for my photographic sessions.

Every morning the editor would riffle through the invitations and parcel them out to us – champagne receptions and trips to the Bahamas for herself, Parker Knoll chairs, Lurex blinds, imaginative uses for kitchen foil, and two hundred ways to tart up tuna for us. Sometimes you got a really wild one like the publicity party for Man Tan, where gorgeous hunks in posing pouches walked around with half of their bodies chalk white and the other half bright orange. I only once managed to land a travel freebie, to Amsterdam for the crowning of Miss Edam Cheese 1958. On £10 a week I could just about afford the occasional pub lunch, but most of the time my co-workers and I lived off the cocktail sausages and canapés laid on at publicity parties.

Apart from shopping, my other job was to answer readers' letters. One had an awful urge to tell them the truth. *Question*: 'I have a Chinese carpet, a striped Regency sofa and a William Morris wallpaper – what should my curtains be?' *Answer*: 'Throw the lot out and start again!' Or, to Mrs M. of Maidstone, who is taking classes in Japanese flower-arranging and fears she is getting too stylised, 'Dear Mrs M., why don't you buy a bunch of daffs and stick them in a jam-jar without taking off the elastic band? You'll feel a whole lot better!'

This trivia took up most of the morning, but after lunch there were long periods when I could sit around pretending to be busy while reading novels under the desk or sticking recipes into my private scrapbook. Then, at six o'clock, there came the ghastly trip home on the No.11 bus in time to read my youngest her bedtime story.

I stuck it for a couple of years, with the magazine becoming more and more trendy – the word 'house' on the cover was getting smaller and smaller and 'wife' bigger and bigger – and a new editor who drove us all a lot harder. I began to find it more and more difficult to give the children the sort of attention I felt they needed. Both they and my work began to suffer as I tried to split myself in two, plagued by guilt and worry.

Gradually I became aware of unpleasant physical symptoms – dry mouth, palpitations and a feeling as if my head was being squeezed by an iron band. Soon after I gave in my notice and went to see my doctor, who diagnosed an incipient nervous breakdown and sent me to see a very eminent psychiatrist. After lots of embarrassing questions he handed me a prescription; 'We don't believe in psycho-analysis here,' he said: 'these pills *work*!' My GP took one look at the prescription and practically fainted. Apart from a strong anti-depressant I was supposed to take a couple of Drinamyl pills a day, the sort of high-powered speed-bombs that they sold in Soho at ten bob a time. Not surprisingly, in no time at all I was feeling absolutely splendid and was permanently as high as a kite. My family called my medication 'Mummy's balmy pills'.

By now the Sixties had started to swing, but in spite of Mr B.'s bombers I was not ready for them. The King's Road was full of Twiggy look-alikes in mini skirts, but I had shot up to eleven stone and was still wearing grey flannel pinafore dresses. With my hair cut short like a boy's and my harlequin spectacles I was a gruesome sight. One night I asked my friend Stephen Vincenzy, who wrote a splendid book called *In Praise of Older Women*, why I was not getting any wolf whistles. 'Well,' he said, 'in the first place that short hair makes you look like a dyke – a *fat* dyke,' he added with brutal honesty. 'And those specs are sheer hell. Lose weight, grow your hair and get some contact lenses!'

At that time the smart thing for fatties was to go to a society doctor called Tony Greenburgh, and have injections of pregnant mare's urine – as a result of which I lost two stone! Contact lenses were easy, as I had got used to wearing those early goldfish bowls when I was in the WAAF, so that only left my hair. Rather than wait months for it to grow I decided to buy a wig – or rather a long hair-piece attached to a velvet head-band, with my own fringe sticking out in front. I thought I looked the cat's whiskers until one day at a party I met April Ashley, England's most gorgeous sex-change. '*Darling!*' she boomed in her penetrating contralto, 'what are you doing with that *lid* on top of your head?' I never wore the dreadful thing again, and six months later my real hair was lapping my shoulders. All that remained was to buy the tightest pair of black trousers in Chelsea, and I was ready for action.

Luckily – and contrary to popular misconception – this was not just a time for the young: people of all ages could have a ball. We may have looked rather silly as we twisted and shook, but we had a bloody marvellous time. Our adrenalin was sky-high, and every day seemed like a new adventure. The music was our life's blood, permeating everything we did – a dramatic sound-track that heightened the most trivial event and made even casual encounters seem like great romances.

We danced by day and by night, not just at clubs but whenever friends dropped in – the record player seemed to be always warm. As for my daughters, they wore a groove in the carpet in front of the loud-speakers learning to do the twist and then the shake.

A lot of the music was fairly banal, but there were certain

songs – 'Layla', 'A Whiter Shade of Pale', 'Nights in White Satin', 'The House of the Rising Sun' – that could send a shiver down your spine. I don't need to mention Dylan, the Beatles and the Stones, because they reigned supreme. It was this music, dancing in our veins and colouring our lives, that made everything seem so much more glamorous than it really was. I know I must have been happy, because time and time again I found myself saying the same thing – 'I want to live for ever!' I even woke up in the morning looking forward to doing the washing-up from the night before.

The King's Road was a wonderful place to be in then. It was full of friendly atmospheric cafés, bars, clubs and restaurants where you could always be sure to run into some member of that amorphous group dreamed up by journalists and known as the Chelsea Set.

On the corner of our square there was an old Victorian eating-house called the Cosy Dining Rooms. It sold bubble and squeak for sixpence and a three-course meal for one and ninepence, and had wooden pews to discourage lingering. For cheap pasta and cappuccinos there was the Picasso, with its hideous fake-Guernica mural. Old-fashioned pubs abounded, with billiard tables and snugs, always full of familiar faces – The Lord Nelson, The Potters, The Six Bells and the Markham Arms. The latter was our favourite, run by old Mrs Andrews who had a cat that played the Wheel of Fortune with its paw. Mrs Andrews would have nothing to do with foreign rubbish like vodka, and charged a penny for a splash of soda.

In the evenings we drank and danced at the Pheasantry or the Arethusa, both within staggering distance of home. The Arethusa was an amazing place, catering for every walk of life, where anything could happen and usually did: one minute you'd be working out on the pitch-black dance floor on your own, the next you might find yourself doing the hitch-hiker with Liberace.

It was here that I first ran into Christine Keeler, a jolly, friendly girl with rabbity teeth – not exactly beautiful, but with great style and very sexy. I used her to distract the barman so that I could nip behind the bar and pinch us both drinks. Our friend Fred Morley, who had a studio in Soho, had taken some very exciting photos of her sitting naked on a black plastic chair, one of which was later to become her trademark.

Every few weeks there'd be a party, and in those days it was always a bottle party with very loud music. Here is a typical run-down on a party given at our house.

In the afternoon collect two large casks of scrumpy from pub in Harrow Road. Wash out large white dustbin and pour it in, ready to be laced with spirits brought by guests.

Pile up bread and cheese on kitchen table.

Hide valuables. Clean floor. Change into white mini dress with huge gilt apples earrings and insert contact lenses.

8 p.m. Switch on enormous secondhand tannoy speaker, and line up tapes and records.

8.15 p.m. Arrival of Aziza the snake dancer, who is to be our cabaret, carrying a BOAC bag containing her python warmed by a hot water bottle.

9 p.m. Blast off with 'I Want to Hold your Hand'. The room goes crazy.

9.30 p.m. First gatecrasher arrives without bottle. He is thrown out by David Litvinoff who works for Rachmann, an evil property tycoon who puts rats painted with fluorescent paint through letter-boxes to flush out sitting tenants.

11 p.m. Aziza does snake dance.

11.30 p.m. Our extrovert friend Mary Rose, who always likes to strip off, emerges naked from behind the curtains with a daffodil between her thighs. Someone is locked in the lavatory with somebody else's wife.

Midnight. Arrival of April Ashley, our beautiful sex change friend, in full evening dress with her train of pretty-boy acolytes. Upstairs, unknown to us, some of David Litvinoff's henchmen are 'doing the overcoats'.

3 a.m. Arrival of the fuzz, called by indignant neighbours – in fact only one rather small and pink-cheeked constable. April swoops down on him, bottle in hand, and bears him away.

4.30 a.m. The fuzz is trying to do the twist with April and feeling no pain. Christine Keeler is dancing on the bar wearing his helmet.

7 a.m. Arrival of Joe the milkman, friend and confidant to

half the street, and the last milkman to keep his horse. The hard core lines up on the balcony to greet him. Some have swopped clothes, some are topless and all are legless. Joe doesn't turn a hair – he's seen it all before.

Last man to leave is novelist Alan Williams, prostrate on the sofa, who is ringing up Fortnum and Mason's and demanding that they send over a crate of champagne – amazingly they do.

By now the room smells like the inside of a very old wine cask, the carpet is sodden, cigarette ends are uncurling in half empty glasses; single earrings and empty bottles litter the floor. Someone has stuffed her sequin jacket behind the storage heater. Somebody whom nobody knows is asleep on the sofa. The party is over.

We soon got the reputation of giving the grooviest parties in Chelsea, though not according to my daughter Camilla. 'Mummy and Daddy gave another of their *boring* parties,' she wrote in her diary: 'not a single man under thirty!'

In fact my two daughters' lives had taken wildly different directions, Clare, the eldest, had been spirited away to a convent by my mother, and was in love with her pony; Cammy, who was strolling around Chelsea in thigh-high white plastic boots, a matelot's cap and lashings of eye-liner, was in love with the Beatles. She looked amazingly mature for her age, and dashing young men in Jags used to roar up to the door demanding to take her dancing at the Arethusa. 'She's only eleven!' I would screech from the balcony; the Jag would roar off again, and I would face recriminations from a tearful and furious Cammy.

Although Clare quite liked her convent, Cammy's London school had not been such a success, as she had fallen under the spell of a female Fagin called Geraldine, whose speciality was 'brickering' – schoolgirl underworld slang for shop-lifting. I would never have known about this if Cammy hadn't taken to leaving notes around the house listing the loot – and not just the things brickered, but their original prices as well. As, for example,

What I pinched from Woollies this hols:
Intimate talcum powder 30/-
Leichner false eyelashes 13/6*d*
Fiona false nails 19/6*d*
Ya Ya lip gloss 10/6*d*
Harriet Hubbard spot cream 12/6*d*.

With nightmare visions of Geraldine brickering merrily down Oxford Street, Cammy trailing behind her with the swag bag and store detectives closing in from all sides, we decided to send her to a new school in the country. Her first letter didn't sound too happy – 'The headmistress is horrid. Very strict and very hard, so is the Arith teacher – she has only got one nostril!' – but at least it was better than brickering.

In 1963, when I reached the ripe old age of forty-two, something strange happened to me: I lost my appetite for raving, and found myself staying at home more and more. Shura, on the other hand, was jetting around Chelsea from one trendy party to another, chatting up birds, while I stayed at home, boringly monogamous.

I didn't particularly relish this situation, for Shura had stopped telling me what party he was going to, and he no longer took me dancing. I began to feel old and no longer 'with it' – just someone for other people to come home drunk to. 'Oh *Joan!*' a hostess was heard to say to a friend of mine: 'I'm afraid she's not here! *Shura's* here, of course, but *Joan* never goes *anywhere!*'

I don't know how or why I got into this situation. The house was always full of people, drinking our booze and pinching my cigarettes, but I felt lonely, an outsider who didn't quite fit in.

The time had obviously come for the worm to turn – and turn it did, with disastrous results.

I should have read my horoscope more carefully. 'Children of Libra, beware!' it muttered ominously, 'Pluto is about to move into your Twelfth House of self-destruction!' In other words, I was about to meet my first psychopath, a man who was to dominate my life for the next five years.

Chapter Six

I was having a drink in The Potter's Arms one day in October 1963 when I noticed a tall, dark young man giving me long meaningful glances from the other side of the bar. As no one had been giving me glances of any kind for quite a long time I was only too happy to bat my false eyelashes in his direction – and, sure enough, he left the group he was with and came looming over. He had piercing hawk-like eyes, an aquiline nose, rather nice dark floppy hair and a weak mouth. He was both good-looking and bad-looking, that fatal combination – a compelling blend of Peter Pan and Captain Hook with a dash of Dracula for good measure. Like all true vampires, he had shown an unerring eye for his victim.

In no time at all we had split – as one used to say – and were baring our souls over cappuccinos at the Kenya Coffee House. His name was John, and apart from being – or so he said – a brilliant artist, he was also apparently the illegitimate son of a noble family, and his early life had been blighted by a cruel and sadistic stepfather. As he was only twenty-seven I was a bit dubious about telling him I was forty-two, but he seemed absolutely thrilled about it – apparently he liked older women.

Knowing that Shura would be out, I asked him home, settled him down with a large drink which seemed to please him enormously, and then fled upstairs to change into my tightest black trousers. This was just as well because when I came down he had already got the Swinging Blue Jeans on the turntable and was doing the 'Hippy Hippy Shake'. I watched his amazing gyrations with my eyes popping out – never had I seen such a mover!

Shortly afterwards, rather to my chagrin, he said he had to go, but slipped an address into my hand. 'Come and have lunch at my studio Sunday,' he murmured.

The 'studio' turned out to be a small, rather scruffy flat off the King's Road which was not even his – he was crashing out with a friend. I began to feel things weren't quite so groovy as I'd thought.

I suppose at this point I could still have escaped, but something about John hypnotised me, and I fancied him something rotten. For the next few weeks we met almost every day, but rather to my surprise and dismay he never offered to kiss me. All he seemed to want to do was to talk, usually about himself. We had illicit meetings at The Red House, a pub next door to the police station. As it was frequented almost exclusively by the fuzz there was no danger of bumping into one's friends.

Unfortunately there is something about a liaison with a younger man which results in instant rejuvenation, and friends saying embarrassing things in front of your husband like 'My God, you look ten years younger! What have you been up to?' I suppose nowadays he'd be called a toy boy – odious phrase! – which gives the impression that the older woman, far from being vulnerable, is in command of the situation. In fact it is much more exciting to be wholly in the power of a tiny tyrant – as I was. By now I felt like I was living inside his head. All his worries and neuroses were mine.

Sometimes, just to put the hook in deeper, he would vanish for a couple of weeks, leaving only a cryptic note –

> 'The woods are lovely dark and deep
> But I have promises to keep
> And miles to go before I sleep.'

Convinced he had left me for ever, I would suffer the pains of an addict whose drug has been suddenly withdrawn. Then he would be back, all smiles, as if nothing had happened, with a gold chain to put about my neck. I had also begun to notice certain things about him. He drank like a fish and began to borrow small sums of money from me – and, even more worrying, he had still not kissed me.

Sometimes he took me dancing and I would feel like a teenager. I wrote in my diary

> *Saturday.* John was wearing a clean blue shirt open at the neck and I could see that he'd been at the sun lamp again. He was so pleased to see me that he fell on his knees. 'God,' he said, 'How I've missed you! There's something I want you to hear!' Then he played me the guitar concerto, so lovely it made my toes curl and afterwards we put on Washington Square and practised the Hitchhiker. Later we went to the Café des Artistes and knocked 'em cold on the dance floor!

One day I said to him jokingly after a couple of drinks, 'You really must meet my husband soon. I think I'll tell him you're queer!' 'Oh,' he said, giving me a puzzled look, 'but I am! Didn't you know?' I looked at him in amazement. 'Then what on earth are you doing here with me?' 'I'm in love with you, of course. I depend on you for every breath I take. I want to be with you always, I never want you to feel lonely again. If we're at a party you need only look across the room at me and you will know I'm there for you. I'm never going to leave you – our time is endless. Hundreds of days, hundreds of nights.'

By now I was totally bemused. Why did he talk about nights? Did he or did he not want to make love to me? I finally plucked up the courage to ask him if he had a boyfriend, and he told me about Kevin – the boy he used to live with, who had broken his heart. 'Kevin was just an illiterate little Irish brat when I met him,' he said bitterly. 'I did a real Pygmalion job on him – smartened him up, taught him to read poetry and what does the ungrateful little bitch do? Walks out on me and pinches all my best clothes into the bargain.'

Now that the cat was out of the bag, John started to talk 'camp', something I suppose he hadn't dared do before. He even let me watch him putting on his 'slap' as he called it, mostly something under the eyes to hide the bags, and a bit of eyeshadow. I was always referred to as 'Maud' or 'Ada', and he used strange words like 'varder' and 'bona' – as in 'Oh Ada, something bona over there is vardering me rotten!' I began to get used to the idea of his being queer – I only wished he didn't radiate such a powerful sexuality!

In desperation I wrote off to my pet astrologist, John Naylor, giving both our birth dates, and asking what he thought of our possible future together. Naylor's reply was brutally frank and to the point:

This man is a broken reed and a clinging vine. At the same time, with his Scorpio flair for drama, he will alternatively raise you up and throw you down until you almost lose your mind. This is a Svengali relationship, and cannot possibly bring you happiness. You will, unless you take firm action, get yourself more deeply involved to your own great and possibly disastrous disadvantage. You are in danger of wrecking your whole world on this relationship. If necessary leave the country! As long as there's a chance of contact he will have you in his grip.

It was a measure of my besottedness that I completely ignored this warning. John was the brother and son that I'd never had, the most dangerous of all incestuous intimacies, and there was no way that I could leave him. I went around looking doomed and interesting. I lost weight and even got down to ten stone, which for me was anorexic. I mooned around listening for hours to Joan Baez on the gramophone wailing on about the young wife who ran away for the demon lover – I suppose in my heart of hearts I still hoped that one day he would make love to me.

On Christmas Eve, I made the mistake of asking John to our Christmas party. We danced together the whole night, and I was wild with excitement and happiness. Shura took one look at my face and went upstairs to pack his bags, and John went down to the kitchen and pretended to cut his wrists with a sliver of broken glass. Both were basically play-acting, but I ended up with a black eye. It was the worst Christmas of my life.

Though deeply worried, Shura was not really in any position to play the heavy husband. As a free-spirited Aquarian he knew all about the allure of wild forays into uncharted territory. He also admitted that the whole thing was partly his fault. If he hadn't neglected me for so long this would never have happened.

'I wrote the script,' he admitted, 'but you have rather over-produced it.'

Wherever the guilt lay, I went on seeing John, and the tension between Shura and me grew worse and worse. We decided that a short separation would be a good thing. Shura, who for several years now had been running a PR company, decided it was time he took a long holiday, and went off to visit friends in Ibiza, while I fled to the South of France with John.

An old lodger of ours, Marye Rouse, gave us a lift in her battered old car which had 'Up The Beatles' and 'Vive La Difference' painted on it. We drove for twenty-four hours without stopping on coffee and cognac, with Marie la Fôret singing about love on the radio.

In the Auberge de Flamande Rose in the Camargue, with a thunderstorm raging overhead and horses snorting and farting in the stalls next door, John and I finally made it. He pinned me down by my wrists on the bed and kissed me for the first time. Then he touched my eyes and my mouth, and stroked my neck and back with strong, blunt fingers, murmuring to me in soft, husky Spanish, the language of love and drunkenness, 'Y tambien, y tambien' – which drove me mad. Little did I know that this was a one-night benefit performance, not to be repeated except on extremely rare occasions. When I tried to kiss him back he averted his face. 'Why do you turn away from me?' I asked. 'Because I'm scared stiff of making love to you. I've been fighting it every inch of the way – didn't you know?'

We sat up for the rest of the night drinking cognac and talking about nostalgic things like dogs and children's books and our childhood fantasies. Mine was to be a British queen like Boadicea dragged in triumph behind a Roman emperor's chariot wheels, but John always dreamed of being raped by an enormous Negro in a leopard skin bikini. As we got drunker we started singing hymns and were still bellowing out 'I Vow to Thee My Country' as the dawn came up. It was a wonderful night.

Next morning we rode along the beach on the famous white horse of the Camargue – nasty, bad-tempered beasts that shied at everything, even water. Another dream shattered! I watched John all the time. He was so beautiful, with his mocking eyes with golden flecks in them, his hair down to his shoulders, self-pitying mouth and a marvellous bottom.

Thursday, 12 March 1964. Our friend Jane Heaton lives in a converted chapel near St Tropez, a Gothic extravaganza with Bach's toccata and fugue echoing round the vaulted ceiling. We arrived to find Jane drinking Pernod and playing back-gammon with her lover Michael, and were given an enormous Napoleonic double bed, and a bidet that shoots out on wheels! We went to bed late. I put out my hand to touch him, and to my amazement he slapped my face hard. 'Keep away, don't touch me! Don't you know how terrible I feel every time I make love to you? When I wake in the morning guilt comes crashing down on to my face like a brazen shield. You want to have your cake and eat it, don't you? You want me for excitement and your husband for security, you two-faced whore.'

Later we made it up, and he said, 'Oh Ada, I do love you but you can't have it both ways – I want you lock, stock and barrel, not in bits and pieces.'

Thursday, 19 March. I am now beginning to see what John is really like, and I am terrified. Once he starts to drink he can't stop. One moment he'll be laughing and friendly, then something seems to go click in his brain and he turns into a different person, a raging, ranting paranoic to whom there is no appeal. I just wait and pray for him to get so drunk that he'll pass out. Michael looks at me pityingly: 'Well, if this is what you want I think you've got it for life. But remember the old Spanish saying – "Take what you want in this world said the Lord, but pay for it."' Then he turned to John and said, 'Why do you hate yourself so much?'

If I'd had any sense I would have packed my bags there and then and taken the next train home. Unfortunately I was now trapped in a new role, that of Florence Nightingale. Even more insidious than the brother/sister intimacy, I was convinced that my mission in life was to save poor John from himself. Saying goodbye to Jane and Michael, who were only too pleased to see us go, we hired a car and set off in the direction of Marseilles. John was drunk and drove through the night like a demon. Ignoring the brakes and driving on the clutch alone he gunned the car round nightmare bends. I thought my last hour had come, but John kept singing 'Esperanza' and telling me to relax, lean back and enjoy it.

Practically all the hotels in Marseilles seemed to be brothels, and ours, The Hotel Pretty, was certainly no exception. Down by the docks, it was in a quarter so sleazy that even the cats made love by daylight.

Sunday, 22 March. John was moody all day. He finally confessed that he needed a boy. 'Here,' he said, 'drink this wine – it'll make you sleep better. I hate to leave you in this shitty place but I'll be back soon. These things don't take long.' As he reached the door he looked back at me. 'Do you realise,' he said, 'this is the first time I've ever left you of my own free will?'

Hours later I was woken by a radiant John. 'Oh Ada, I've been drinking with the entire Israeli navy! They're the most wonderful people I've ever met. I spotted them in the Bar Frou-Frou, all these gorgeous creatures drinking and singing and hugging and kissing each other, but not all queer, just affectionate. And this boy Jakov – such beautiful long lashes – came over and sat on my knee. I'm meeting him tomorrow at the end of the gangplank.'

Two weeks later John left for Israel – not because of Jakov, but because of what Jakov had told him about the country. He seemed to think it would be his salvation. We said goodbye in a Spanish seamen's bar full of artificial flowers and bullfighter dolls, playing Edith Piaf on the jukebox and getting drunk on cheap brandy. 'Do you realise,' John said, 'that every one of these chaps playing cards is waiting to see if I can walk away from the bar after ten brandies? This is one of the best drunks I've had in years, and one of the happiest afternoons of my life.' He sprinkled me with water and wine: 'It's an old Spanish custom – it means the person you do it to is the dearest thing to you after God.' Next day he sailed for Israel.

I came home to find Shura already back from Ibiza. He said he had been worried sick about me the whole time he'd been away. He saw John as a kind of blood-sucking monster, and me as his victim and dupe, but he felt sure that one day this thing would burn itself out and that I'd come back to earth again. 'Don't worry,' he said, 'I'll never desert you. I'm not the sort of ship that leaves the sinking rat!'

When John came back from Israel six months later he was a new man – strong and fit, free from paranoia and, above all, sober. With £300 I had lent him he bought a ramshackle old manor house in the north of Scotland, and planned to farm the land. In the meantime he was painting like crazy in a Notting Hill Gate studio. I felt like the self-satisfied mother of a Mongol child that was showing unusual progress.

It was too good to last. One night, going to meet John for a quiet supper, I heard the sounds of screams, oaths and splintering glass. Peering nervously round the door, I saw John in the process of breaking up the studio.

'That little bitch Kevin's back in town!' he sobbed. 'I ran into him in the Earl's Court Road and he cut me dead!' Another glass hurtled across the room, ricocheted off the stove and hit me on the forehead, causing a nasty gash.

'Oh my God!' John groaned, clutching his head, 'everyone's going to think I did it – I'd better call my solicitor!'

'Call a doctor, more likely,' I snapped. He took me to St Mary Abbot's, where they put in five stitches. I was in no state to go home, so slipped into bed beside John.

Next morning we heard someone ringing the front doorbell and the landlord answering it. A beautiful boy with a face of an angelic street urchin came in without knocking. He approached the bed gingerly, crunching on broken glass and kicking aside blood-stained clothing. I dived under the covers.

'Kevin!' gasped John. 'For three years I've been waiting for you to turn up, and you have to pick on this particular morning.'

'Bad timing, eh?' Kevin said with a satisfied smirk. 'And

what do you think you're doing, eh? Playing at lesbians?' He looked with distaste at the wrecked flat. 'Violence too, I see! Well, that's a turn-up for the books – I always thought of you as a masochist.'

By now John had pulled himself together. 'Well, Heather, as you're here you might as well make us some breakfast. Go on, get your skates on you grotty little Irish Ted, there's a sliced loaf and some Oxford Marmalade in the kitchen.'

I lay in bed eating toast and marmalade and listening to a radiantly happy John telling Kevin all about Sweeney House in Scotland. 'Why don't you come up there with me? There's lots to do, we could get grants and farm the land together. You wouldn't mind a bit of hard work, would you? We'd have the place on wheels in no time!'

My heart leapt with excitement. For the first time I could feel the vulture on my wrist shifting its heavy claws from side to side, and preparing for flight. I still wanted John in my life – I just didn't want him around all the time. I was totally hooked on the main drama, but I no longer cared if I was the heroine or the chambermaid provided I was not left out of the play.

Friday, 1 May. John is triumphantly happy in Scotland with Kevin. Sweeney House is great, he crows – hi-fi from wall to wall, and Dimple Haig from floor to ceiling. He and Kevin are hard at work converting and decorating what they still ironically refer to as 'your house'. Euphoric letters pour in every few days.

Monday, 11 May. 'Joan darling, I am so happy and so grateful. I can't wait to show you Sweeney! I want to see you walking through the iron gates up the drive and through the garden into the panelled hall. You will think it the most beautiful house you've ever seen! Then I want you to walk down to the sea with the wind making your face burn to this fantastic coast right at the bottom of our garden. You can sit on the short-cropped turf and look down into a blue-black chasm below where seals swim and cormorants dive. Then back for tea with strawberry jam and a huge black iron kettle on the stove. Upstairs I'd have made up the big brass bedstead with coarse linen sheets, cold to the touch. Don't you long to wake up in that bedroom on a fresh summer's day, hearing the wind tear through the long grass in the orchard like a knife going through rough silk? This is the house of both our childhoods – every fantasy is there. The panelled hall, the stone stairs, the trunks in the attic, the dairy and the hooks for hanging game. I love it here, I love water, sky, stone, earth and leaves – I never want to live in that sewer London again!

'Do you like the new Marianne Faithfull record? I think it's fab. Kevin's favourite is "Moon River", he plays it all the time. He is very happy and contented here and doesn't pine for the bright lights or for anyone else but me. I could never ask him to leave, he belongs here too. Like me he feels safe at last. You must never be jealous of him. He fills all the gaps that you can never fill because of your family – Kevin is my family. Needless to say, to avoid scenes we'll all be sleeping "tout seul" when you come in July!'

Friday, 22 May. 'Darling, got up at six and saw the dawn in, sitting on my favourite gate. The sea was Mediterranean blue, the mountains had snow on them – there were goldfinches flashing past and skylarks singing. I couldn't have felt closer to God if I tried, – there was even a niche in the wall to hold my whisky glass. Dawn is such a super time to get pissed. The only terrifying thing was that I suddenly couldn't visualise life without you – even if we only see each other for a few weeks a year. I don't think I'd know what to do without you, life would just stop and become infinitely empty if you weren't in it. I suppose you couldn't adopt me, could you?'

Monday, 25 May. 'Oh Ada, what a week! Ploughed the field, painted the gate, cleaned out the out-buildings and creosoted all the wood. Stripped down all rooms ready for painting – it's so exciting I want to ring you every hour to tell you of our latest achievement. Our grant should come through any day now. We're planning a market garden with greenhouses. It's all going to be much cheaper and easier than we thought, but could you send me a little money for fags meanwhile? Love you always, John.'

As you can imagine all this made me very thrilled and happy. The vampire still loved me, but he was off my neck and on to somebody else's, and jolly good luck to both of them. At least he was happy, working hard and forming a new relationship. Unfortunately Kevin, a streetwise boy, was already beginning to feel uneasy about the whole set-up. Money was running out, there was still no sign of a grant, and he was getting restless.

Monday, 1 June. 'Darling, Kevin is being difficult! One moment he says he's in love with me, the next that living together won't work and he's leaving, and two hours later we're in bed together! All this emotional strain is driving me to the bottle, and that sends him into deeper sulks, going around with his head down like a little bull. It's awfully boring. Last week I lost my temper and gave him a black eye, which has now gone a nice shade of purple and Naples yellow. Thank God he's found a book to read, that will keep him quiet for a few days as he can only read about a page an hour.

'Oh, did I tell you about the midnight sun? It's super but the awful thing is you never know when it's bedtime so you never know when to stop drinking – which reminds me, hold on a sec while I get a dram.

'Went upstairs to get the booze and I see that your portrait, which used to be on the bedroom wall, is now on the staircase! In six months' time you'll probably be in the elsan. Oh yes, and another thing, I caught K. doing up one of the old sheds. He says it's for you to sleep in when you come down in July. He's christened it the Dower House – cheeky bugger. I think K. and I are due for a little heart to heart tonight.'

A few weeks later John and Kevin heard from the council that their grant had been turned down. That night Kevin wrote a letter to his good friend, pop star Long John Baldry: 'Dear John, This empire has well and truly fallen. For Christ's sake get me out of here! You can send me my fare to the Lybster Post Office.'

In July I was working as a cook at the Bird's Nest, a rather up-market fish and chip caff in Cornwall. I fried all day and slept over the shop at night. Later that month I was due to visit the happy couple in Scotland and see Sweeney House for the first time. Then one morning at 3 a.m. the phone rang, and I heard John's desperate voice, choked with tears. 'He's gone – he's walked out! For God's sake come up right away – I can't cope on my own.'

I rang up Shura in London and told him I had to go to Scotland for a bit on a matter of urgency. Shura quite under-stood – he was in fact rather fond of John by this time, and desperately sorry for him. I promised to keep in touch and not take any unnecessary risks.

John met me at the station – unshaven, covered in scars, skeletal – and drove me to Sweeney. I hated the house from the minute I set eyes on it. It stood, stark and lonely, on the cliff's edge – a fine house, but unsoftened by any surrounding greenery, like something out of a horror film. It was open to the winds and to the prying eyes of the nearby villagers, whom one could visualise creeping about on all fours behind their garden walls with binoculars, hoping to catch a glimpse of what those weird buggers at the House were up to. John took one look at my face and knew that I hated it. He did everything he could to make me feel at home, bringing me tea on a tray with Tiptree strawberry jam. All night long I could hear him hammering away, putting up pictures and arranging a desk for me with blotting pad and photographs – lures to make me stay.

Next night he vanished, coming back long after I was in bed with three drunken fishermen. They danced around my bed waving live crabs over me and singing in Gaelic. After they'd gone John, who was paralytically drunk, knelt by the wall, knocking his head rhythmically against it and crying 'Why me, God, why me? I don't ask much, do I? Just the total oblivion of four walls and a bottle and someone to love me – just someone warm and breathing near me, someone always there, someone to come home to. I don't care whether it's a man or a woman or a dog, provided it's mine and mine alone. Love is need and need is love. That's what love means, and all the troubadors and high towers and fluttering scarves add up to nothing else.'

Thursday, 16 July. John has deteriorated further, with terrible pains in his head. He can't stop crying and is drinking like a fish. He seems to be in a constant state of nameless terror. 'I've always known I was mad,' he'd tell me. 'I've known it since the age of ten. I just can't cope with life or with people, so I open my mouth and scream for help like a child lost in a traffic jam.'

All he needs is someone to hold him tight when he feels the madness coming on and tell him 'It's all right, John, you're alive, you're on earth, you're not going to turn into something horrible and be lost in darkness.' But there's no one – Kevin has gone, and I can't carry this burden much longer. It's like thrashing in an icy sea with a drowning man clinging to my neck. I don't think I love John any more – it's just pity and a deep affection. My own mind is crystal clear. I wake up in the morning, sweep up the broken glass, wash the blood from the walls and the vomit from the stairs, feed the dog, put on the kettle and life goes on – I shall survive.

Tomorrow I am taking John to the psychiatric clinic in Edinburgh to see my friend Mrs Janson, who is a nurse there. She says we can stay with her a couple of days while he gets treatment.

Saturday, 18 July. Everything was going well, J. very sweet and co-operative. I left him at the clinic and went for a walk up to the castle. It was a beautiful sunny day with a biting wind, and I decided to visit my lecturer friend, Ralph. He says I can always stay with him if things turn sour, but I told him everything was going to be all right. I walked back in the cold sunshine feeling happy and hopeful for the first time in weeks.

I ran upstairs calling John's name, threw open the bed-room door and was confronted by an ugly stranger, a face contorted with hate, the eyes narrow and lips curled back in a mocking snarl. Peter Pan had flown away, and Captain Hook – mad, bad and dangerous to know – was standing by the fireplace, drinking brandy out of a toothmug.

'It was you, wasn't it?' he hissed. 'You were the reason Kevin left me! I've been working it out all afternoon. He knew you'd be coming to the house soon, and he just couldn't take it. You wanted to see the house, did you? Wanted to screw me more likely, you two-faced bitch! Why couldn't you have left us alone? We were so happy!'

He reached for the brandy bottle again and I knew the violence would start soon. I made a dash for the door, but he was there before me, kicking me and lashing out with his fists. My screams brought Mrs Janson up. 'Get out of here, you monster!' she declaimed in a melodramatic voice – which had the desired effect of getting John out of the front door. For half an hour the bell did its three chimes and the dog barked. Then the police came, and John left on the next train to London.

Mrs Janson bathed my eye and made me a nice cup of tea. 'You better be careful, dear,' she said. 'The pain he feels is real, the loneliness and need are real, but the danger to you is also very real.'

I was in no position to go home with a black eye – and, as always, my first thought was to protect the attacker, like a vampire's victim who hides the puncture marks on his neck. I thought I would find a safe, quiet refuge with my friend Ralph for a day or two until my eye had faded – but it was not to be.

As soon as supper was over Ralph disappeared behind a screen and leapt out in a black Merry Widow corset with red suspenders. Oh shit, I thought, not another one! I raced to my room and locked the door, hoping for some peace and quiet and a nice long lie-in, only to be blasted out of my bed next morning by a gun which was stationed on the Castle wall just outside my window. There was nothing for it but to go home and pretend I'd been knocked over by a bike.

During the next few weeks pathetic letters of apology arrived: 'I feel like a dirty old rag doll in a corner, unwanted and torn,

never to be picked up and played with again. Every time I think
of you I can only remember your back and my eyes following
you down some strange street as you run back to normality.
The horrible thing is that you are my normality. I am nothing
and no one without you. My greatest wish is to have a relationship with you without guilt or dramas, one where we can walk
round London free from gossip and I can look your husband
and family in the face.'

Needless to say I forgave him. Shortly afterwards, to my
immense relief, he went off to teach in a boys' college in
Switzerland. As for Sweeney House, he never wanted to see it
again, so I flogged it off as quickly as possible for £2,000.

Now things were once again as I wanted them. I was still loved,
still part of the play, but the succubus was off my back. It was
time to get back to work.

Luckily our friend Michael Alexander – always referred to
in the gossip columns as 'a leader of the Chelsea Set' – had
decided to open a restaurant and offered me the job of cooking
in an extraordinary establishment known as The Gasworks, just
beyond World's End.

A workmen's café by the gasometer, it was run by a splendid
character known as Jack 'The Lad' Leach, who had covered
every inch of the walls and ceiling with bric-à-brac and fake old
masters – or, as he put it 'Well, not exactly fake, just a bit
schneid, as you might say.' Jack was nothing if not flash – he
carried a gold-plated cosh and drove an open Rolls Royce.
Sometimes, as I was walking sedately to work down the King's
Road, Jack's Roller would roar to a halt beside me and I'd hear
a bellow of ' 'ello, Princess, comin' down to the piss-ole?'

I had two frightfully grand co-cooks called Grosvenor and
Cavendish, known to the customers as 'the Squares'. During
the day the café was an interesting cross-section of society. At
the back, debs were cooking Irish stew and fish pie, at the
counter Jack's wife Shirl was pouring tea for the gas workers,
in the front villains were plotting. It was some time before the
groups mingled, but one day when I was making shepherds'
pie – I always seemed to be making shepherds' pie – a cherubic-

looking character called Socko Sweeney sidled into my kitchen and asked if I had anything that looked like blood. Apparently some gang wanted him to seriously incapacitate a fellow mobster who had got up their noses. Unfortunately this character was a friend of Socko's, so he planned to grab the £50 and fake the assault. After a lengthy search through the store cupboard for the right colour, we finally fell back on good old Heinz tomato ketchup.

After that Socko became a firm friend and we spent many happy hours chatting. Among his many endearing attributes – apparently – was the biggest plonker in Chelsea, on which he could balance two pints of beer. He also had a matchbox in his pocket containing a human ear, bitten off a barman who had refused to serve him, and Ronnie Kray's teethmarks in his scalp. ''e was giving me aggro,' he explained, 'so I went in with me nut!'

Come evening, the Gasworks was transformed into a smart bistro. The candles were lit, the Monkees thundered from the jukebox and I started serving a thirty-shilling three-course meal from behind the counter. We had no licence, so the wine – a lethal brew known as G.B.H. white or red, which came in plastic barrels – was thrown in for free, which was probably not strictly legal.

The next person to arrive was our head waitress, the trans-sexual April Ashley, magnificent in black satin and pearls. Coq au vin was always a popular choice on the menu, as it enabled April to say things like 'What on earth has become of my coq?' This was much appreciated by the punters – mostly Chelsea types who thought they were slumming. Jack was extremely scornful of the clientele, particularly the more upper-crust ones. 'Wot a cunt!' he used to cry, pointing at some unfortunate young aristo picking at his shepherds' pie: 'It's stamped all over 'im, innit, like the little lion on the eggs!'

About midnight we all knock off and finish up the leftovers, while the manager checked the till for fiddling.

It was a pleasant job and I could happily have carried on indefinitely, but unfortunately Michael had other ideas. One night I overheard him out front chatting up some loathsome little pillock who fancied himself as a chef. '*Yes*,' I heard Michael say enthusiastically, '*poussin* stuffed with grapes and flambéd in Calvados – that's *exactly* what this place needs!'

I got roaring drunk on G.B.H. and, according to April, was spotted crawling from hotplate to hatch on all fours. 'Phone for the fish knives, Norman!' she intoned, 'Cook is a little unnerved!'

A few weeks later I quit the Gasworks, little knowing that, back on the home front, fate was about to deal me a cruel double blow.

I was sitting happily watching 'Gardeners' World' when the phone rang.

'This is Mrs Chesham-Smythe speaking, Camilla's head-mistress. I'm afraid I have some bad news for you. Camilla is being sent home.'

'You mean for the weekend?'

'No, Mrs Shivarg, for good. We have found she has *certain tendencies* – not to put too fine a point on it, she has been discovered in bed with a junior!'

I was struck dumb. Did this total idiot actually think that my thoroughly normal, boy-mad daughter was a lesbian?

'Of course she tried to explain it away,' Mrs Chesham-Smythe ground on. 'She says the child was frightened during a thunderstorm and thought she saw her mother's ghost. But we know better. There's also the matter of her unsuitable clothes and make-up, and this indecent book that we found in her locker called *The Pursuit of Love*.'

'But isn't that by – '

'Please don't interrupt, Mrs Shivarg – I've not been head-mistress for thirty years for nothing. And that is not all, I fear. When Miss Browlock, her house mistress, went to the san. to talk to Camilla about her little tendencies, your daughter hit her over the head with her guitar!'

Oh good girl, I thought, bully for you! But I realised her goose was well and truly cooked.

Next morning, while still reeling from the shock, I got a call from John in Switzerland.

'Ada, I've been sacked!'

'You what?'

'Well, they ran some routine blood tests the other day and they seem to think I've got the clap!'

'But have you? I mean *could you*?'

'It seems terribly unlikely. I've been awfully good with the boys – but there *was* that lion tamer in Venice – '

Both my delinquent offspring turned up the next day within hours of each other, both totally devastated. I had made a cheese soufflé to take my mind off things, but no one had any appetite.

John, of course, had nowhere to stay, so the family offered to put him up for a few days in the little room under the stairs that used to be a loo. I knew that once he was in it he would be there for ever, but there was nothing I could do. For years I had made the mistake of plugging the image of 'good' John, while covering up for 'bad' John. By now the whole family was quite fond of him and the cuckoo had come home to roost. Meanwhile Shura had opened a Peking restaurant called The Golden Duck in Hollywood Road, which not only gave us some great free meals, but also enabled him to practise his Mandarin; and Cammy, for whom we had had to find a new school, found herself taking her A-levels at a London comprehensive, which she hated. Although it had been highly recommended to us by a teacher friend, the level of education was fairly abysmal. Most of the boys were more interested in shooting lead pellets into the science master's wooden leg than in acquiring learning.

Three months later – by now it was the summer of 1968 – John was still with us, needless to say. He had achieved his greatest ambition – living with me full-time in a completely guilt-free situation, with no question of sex and unlimited opportunities for bumming free drinks and fags off me. Even so I can't pretend it wasn't a happy time. There is something very cosy and companionable about living with a homosexual with whom one can gossip and talk about hair and make-up. Every morning John ironed a spotless pair of skin-tight jeans, put on a touch of mascara , stuck in the Carmen rollers and admired his bottom in front of my long mirror. We had a lot of laughs. If it hadn't been for John's sense of humour I would have chucked him out months before, especially as he started borrowing money from me again. It's one thing to be a vampire's victim, quite another to be his bank manager.

Round about six, if he hadn't succeeded in scrounging any

money from me – he referred to it as 'change', as if that made it sound less serious – he went in for an operation known as 'doing the overcoats'. This involved a quick search through all the pockets in the hall, which usually yielded him the four bob necessary to buy a beer at the Arethusa Club. From there on he could rely on friends to buy him rounds.

Sometimes, if he was very flush from doing what he called a 'jobette', he went to the Jermyn Street Turkish Baths, picked up a boy and didn't come back until breakfast time: but most nights he got drunk on his own, listening to Tchaikovsky or Dvorak and passing out on the sofa as the dawn chorus began to stir in the trees outside. Often I found an almost illegible note on my desk in the morning: 'I love you – I wish I could live with you forever. I wish you were me, I wish I was you, like one enormous ingrowing toenail! I wish that only you and I existed.'

He was determined to please me at all costs, and devised unexpected flights to Never-Never Land – breakfasting at dawn in the New Forest, drinking wine and eating cold pizza among the wild ponies, watching the sun come up from a bed of bee orchids, bracken and bog myrtle.

Another night in the Arethusa Club, while Shura was away in the country, I casually mentioned to John that I was reading *Tess of the D'Urbevilles,* but had never been to Hardy country. Although it was then two in the morning, he borrowed a car from a friend and by daylight we were standing on a cliff top in Dorset. 'You see,' he said, as we wandered over the hills together, 'I always give you what you want in the end!' (Take what you want, said the Lord, but pay for it.)

He booked us into a little guesthouse where we had an idyllic dinner, but afterwards he went off to Portsmouth and got beaten up by sailors. Whenever I was with him I felt half-ecstatic and half-terrified – even at the most delightful moments there was always a whiff of gunpowder in the air.

Three months later the keg finally exploded. I'd made the grave error of hiding my diaries in the cupboard next to where John slept. The early ones included all of my doubts and fears about him, and a detailed analysis of why I considered him a psychopath – in particular his inability to feel real love.

One night, after drinking half a bottle of brandy, he burst

into the sitting-room holding a diary out at arm's length, as if he could hardly bear to touch it.

'And what pray, madam, might this be?' (He always talked like a stage villain when violence was in the air.)

I got up to run but he pushed me back and pulled a knife out of his pocket. I went cold with terror.

'So I'm a psychopath, am I? Well in that case I'd better start behaving like one.'

He took down his portrait of me, which was hanging over the fireplace, hacked out the canvas and rammed the frame down around my neck. As he came towards me with the knife I thought This is it – he's finally going to kill me. Instead he began tracing the lines on my face with the point of the knife.

'Don't worry,' he sneered, 'I don't hurt old ladies. And you *are* old, aren't you? You look about sixty tonight. You've got lines *here*, and *here* and *here* – no, don't flinch or I'll cut you.'

The knife point ran icily from nose to mouth and across my forehead. Then something seemed to break inside him and he began to cry.

'Oh Ada, how could you say I didn't love you? I didn't mind you calling me a drunk and a queer and a psychopath, but to say that *I can't love*! Don't you know that love has wrecked my whole life?'

I heard the front door bang behind him, and a few minutes later a brick came through the window. This time there was no cover-up. It was the end of John, who was banned from the house.

Over the next few years he would occasionally come to the front door, mainly to beg the price of a drink or his fare home to his mother in the country. At first it was a few shillings, then it went up to a pound and finally to £5. We reckoned we could measure the rate of inflation by how much it took to get rid of him.

Of course I pined for him occasionally, and even thought it might be possible to see him sometimes as a casual friend. 'Casual friendship with *John*,' said my husband in disbelief: 'you might as well try to dance a minuet with an octopus!'

Many years later I was passing a building site in Earl's Court and stopped to ask the way. 'Hold on a sec,' said the foreman, 'I'll just ask me mate.' A brown figure, stripped to the waist, lowered his pick-axe and I saw again those hooded eyes and that twisted mouth, and for a moment was swept by a wave of nostalgia. Then common sense took over, and I turned and fled. Behind me I could hear the foreman's puzzled voice. 'Some funny old lady asking the way ... That's odd, she seems to have disappeared!' ❧

Chapter Seven

During the years that I had spent with the vampire, Shura had been unflaggingly loyal and supportive – not just because he loved me but because he realised I was totally out of control, off my trolley and out to lunch, and he didn't want to see me go down the tubes. Apparently I was suffering from something known as 'folie à deux'.

Luckily we had no difficulty in patching things up – the John episode had, if anything, served to bring us closer together – but there were a few loose ends to take care of. During the worst period Shura had naturally sought comfort in the company of other women, and one in particular known to the family as the Crocodile. She was a sort of mistress that every wife who wished to cement her marriage should get by mail order. Here is a typical evening *chez* la Croc.

11 p.m. Husband suddenly decides he has had enough and wants to go home to his wife but cannot find either his trousers or his car keys. Croc has stuffed his trousers into the deep freeze, and thrown the keys out of the window, and is now sitting up in bed roaring with laughter. Husband – who now has the bit between his teeth – climbs out of the window clutching an umbrella, edges precariously along the sill, trying not to look down at the four-storey drop, and bangs on the lighted window next door. The blind shoots up to reveal a Pakistani family disturbed at a late supper, dumbfounded by the sight of a stranger in his underpants brandishing an umbrella. As

the blind shoots down again the Crocodile sinks her teeth into his calf, practically sending him hurtling down to his death.

It is this sort of episode that makes a man appreciate the quiet pleasures of home. And in fact home was now a pretty pleasant place. We had two half-Siamese kittens, thanks to a follower of the Maharaji, a plump twelve-year-old who claimed to be divine. The disciple had flown away with the Maharaji to India on his Divine Jumbo Jet, leaving us with a pregnant Siamese cat, two of whose litter we kept. We also had two very nice lodgers, Mary Killen and Kerry Kohler, and the thatched cottage in the country left to us by my mother, who had sadly died a few years before.

The cottage was still very beautiful, but it had changed a lot since my mother's day. The farmyard was full of battery hens, the old blacksmith's forge had become the Forge Garage, and our nice neighbour, old Miss Lofts, who used to toddle over to take tea with my mother, had been replaced by a second-hand car-dealer with rottweilers.

The cottage, once full of lovely old furniture, had been burgled in full daylight of practically everything of value, including the grandfather clock.

For weeks afterwards my husband slept with a motley array of weapons by his bedside, including a flick knife, a mallet, a .22 revolver and a Mace gun – (one of those American sprays used by police on rioters to temporarily blind them and mark them with orange dye).

One Whitsun morning he absent-mindedly pocketed the spray and went down to the garden to plant a tree. As he dug in, the spade's handle activated the gun which directed a lethal spray in the general direction of his crotch. Blinded with pain he rushed into the bathroom, knocking his eye on the corner of the medicine cabinet, and turned up on Tuesday morning at Dr Thomas's surgery with orange balls and a black eye.

'My goodness, Mr Shivarg,' observed our unflappable GP, 'you do seem to have spent an interesting and unusual bank holiday!'

One of the few good things which the burglars missed was a sixteenth-century chest containing all my mother's treasured dressing-up things, which we used to play with as children. Kerry, who was studying at the Royal College of Art Film

School, fell on them gleefully and decided we should make films.

Our first film, *Dracula* – in which I played a depraved Mother Superior – was a great success, though judging from the shooting script it was a mite unsubtle:

1 Mad monk rises from grave and
2 Bites Joan
3 Bites Camilla
4 Camilla bites Kerry
5 Kerry bites Mary
6 Mary bites Joan
7 Joan is hacked to death in chapel
8 Kerry is bludgeoned to death with crucifix (blood on walls)
9 Mary runs hysterically through garden and is impaled.

With everything at home going smoothly, I now felt I was ready for a new job.

It was Jeremy Beadle who first told me about the Bickershaw pop festival in Lancashire which he was helping to organise. We were down at the cottage, where Jeremy, a natural clown, had been freaking out the inhabitants of Wendover with his surreal antics at local fêtes and jumble sales. It was going to be a fantastic festival, he said, with the Grateful Dead coming over to play, and before I knew it he had talked me into running a food tent.

My next move was to find a partner, and one night in Finch's I had the good luck to run into a tall, thin fellow with hair down to his shoulders, called Mr Submarine Man. He ran an American sandwich shop and could get more coleslaw out of a cabbage than anyone else in the business.

Apart from his sandwiches we planned to have great vats of steaming soup and a bean stew. Together we scoured scrap yards and found plenty of old saucepans and a huge iron cauldron for my stew, but we still didn't have enough money for all the ingredients. It was Mr Submarine Man who had the brilliant idea that we should approach Maggi Soups and ask them to sponsor us.

An extremely suave PR man took me out to lunch and agreed

to supply us with 200 tins of Maggi soup powder provided I
wore a mob-cap and an apron and called my tent Maggi May's
Soup Kitchen. I managed to wriggle out of the cap and apron
somehow, and we clinched the deal. I hired four Calor gas
boilers and a twenty-foot tent, and we were in business. My
work force consisted of me, my daughter, Kerry, Mr Submarine
and his tribe of children, plus two vegans from Dorset called
Goat and Pilgrim. They were having serious marital problems
because she has erotic dreams about hamburgers.

Friday, 12 May 1972. Freezing cold and pissing with rain.
We have managed to get bales of hay from the local farmer
which are excellent as wind breaks, and also, when loosened,
to sleep under. The communal loos are already indescribable.
You sit balanced over a sort of pit, not daring to look down,
and to make matters worse the doors don't close.

   Oxtail and tomato soup is already bubbling away in the
boilers – our motto is 'Bickershaw Mud and Bickershaw
Blood – Get Them Here!'

   I have started a dried bean stew in the cauldron. I'm
wearing a red cotton Indian skirt and boots and have no
intention of taking either off for the duration. If soldiers can
sleep in their boots, so can I. The rain is still coming down
and the mud is six inches deep around the tent. Even in the
sleeping bag and with a bale of hay thrown over me I am still
powerfully cold and shake all night. Luckily Kerry remembered to bring a bottle of whisky.

Saturday, 13 May. Sunlight coming through the tent door.
Goat woke first and confided to me that she'd dreamt of a
giant hamburger in a Nazi helmet chasing her down Battersea
High Street. Pilgrim, whose vegan diet was big on beans, was
waking with a series of mild rippling farts, muffled luckily by
his sleeping-bag. Easing his pale spidery legs out of the bag
he yawned, stretched and assumed the yoga posture known
as the Standing Crane.

   We made ourselves some tea on one of the small Calor gas
burners and got ready for the hungry hippies – or freaks, as
they like to call themselves now – who are lining up outside

with their rallying cry of 'Twenty pee? It's a rip-off!' My stew is bubbling on, but the beans are still rock hard – I'm getting worried.

A whole village of tents and marquees has grown up around us in the night. People are squatting round their morning camp fires and Jesus Freaks are marching through the camp site singing 'Jesus Wants Me for a Sunbeam'. I can hear the music starting up from the big stage just below us.

It's getting dark now and the camp fires are beginning to glow all over the fields. The stage is a blazing arena surrounded by myriads of tents, their banners fluttering in the wind. The silhouettes of giant lighting towers loom up like siege engines. The Grateful Dead, after two hours of tuning up, are finally pounding away on stage, the sounds roaring from the huge speakers.

Back in the tent I noticed a terrible smell and tracked it down to the iron cauldron – Oh God, I thought, my bean stew has fermented! Mr Submarine Man, who was busy churning out coleslaw, came over and peered dubiously into the turgid depths. 'Hot rats' teeth,' he muttered, 'it's moving! We'd better dump it in the ditch before we all suffocate.'

With the help of Pilgrim he manhandled the huge pot out of the tent and staggered with it towards a ditch where two unsuspecting Indian cooks from the nearby Ashram tent were having a nap. They were woken by a lava-like flow of hot fermenting bean stew, and fled in a flurry of oriental oaths, shaking dried beans out of their turbans.

This however was not the last disaster of the evening. I was listening to Captain Beefheart when a sudden surge in the crowd threw me up against the wire fence in front of the stage, where I slipped and fell under the feet of the rampaging fans. Luckily I escaped with a badly sprained wrist, and was carted off by ambulance to the local out-patients, having been issued with an extremely sinister pink pass that said 'J. Shivarg, DESTROY ON RE-ENTRY'.

Sunday, 14 May. Here I am, arm in plaster, doing my old Mother Courage act with the Maggi soups, which by now are getting embarrassingly lumpy. Where the hell are my helpers? A quick search reveals several feet sticking out below the trestle table, where half the 'staff' are tripping out on California Sunshine.

Monday, 15 May. Everyone has gone, but not us because we are stuck in the mud. Mr Submarine has gone off into Alram to get a tow. Luckily we still have one small primus stove, a bottle of whisky, some Nescafé and a few tins of pineapple juice. The water has been cut off but we have made a wonderful brew of coffee boiled up with the juice and laced with whisky – a kind of Caribbean version of Irish coffee.

We've got the money – what there is of it – in sacks at the back of the tent with Kerry sitting firmly on it, as looters are prowling around picking up plastic bags of hamburger buns and old copies of *Frendz* and *I.T.* The whole site is a sea of mud like a First World War battlefield, with smoke curling up from dying fires and sheets of silvery polythene shining like hoar frost. We reckon that after we've knocked off our expenses we've made a grand profit of about thirty quid!

Still, it didn't matter – I'd had a wonderful time, and I wouldn't have missed it for anything. Sadly I walked down to watch the stage being dismantled, feeling filthy and exhausted but wild and free as a gypsy. Or rather I did until one of the workmen whistled at me, and – much to my rage – called out 'Silly old moo!'

Mr Submarine wants us to do Lincoln – but I think perhaps I've had enough of cold and discomfort.

You may well ask why I let myself in for all these unrewarding culinary adventures – pop festivals, grotty caffs and the like. The fact is I loved cooking, company and conversation, and as no self-respecting posh restaurant was going to let me near its kitchens I had to fall back on what's known as 'alternative catering': easygoing, semi-amateur joints that might be a bit on the squalid side but were enormous fun to work in. I always found that the best friendships were forged under acute stress – people working together under horrible conditions have a unique kind of camaraderie, rather like in the Blitz.

This was certainly true of Etcetera, a kind of semi-health

food place which I ran in the Portobello Road – at the more colourful end where the fruit and veg stalls are, just opposite Ceres Wholefoods.

You went through an old clothes shop and found yourself in a small room with church pews, wooden tables and a bar behind which I cooked mainly vegetarian food. I think this must have been in the early Seventies because I can remember changing brown rice and veg on the blackboard from five bob to twenty-five pee. Our prices were rock-bottom, but this did not stop the local layabouts from writing things like 'Just another trendy rip-off' on the loo walls.

Our customers fell roughly into four categories – smart tourists and Americans who picked dubiously at my lentil pancakes but felt they were lapping up the local colour, characters in Kaftans with bells round their ankles who sat all day over a bowl of brown rice, using their own chopsticks, serious health freaks from Ceres across the road, and the real no-hopers who carried their change in matchboxes. 'Wot 'ave you got for two pee?' was one of their favourite gambits. If this didn't work they frequently pinched money from the tips saucer, which we rather foolishly kept on the counter.

I made no money out of Etcetera, but I loved it just the same. I would unlock the door in the morning and stand there breathing in the familiar fragrance of stale coffee, incense sticks and mouse droppings, and I'd feel really happy and at home.

To make some extra money I also worked evenings at a restaurant called Zog run by my writer friend Bill Hopkins, one of the original 'angries'.

One day I came in to find Bill looking unusually smug and pleased with himself. 'I've got this wonderful new chef,' he told me enthusiastically, '– Monsieur Gustav from Lyons.'

An amazing apparition, all in white and wearing a chef's hat popped up like Hamlet's father's ghost from behind the bar, and to my astonishment I recognised Gus, my old cook from La Roma in Oxford – he who used to sling spaghetti at the wall to see if it was done. 'Gus!' I was about to screech when the apparition put a finger to its lips. Bill suggested that I show Monsieur Gustav the kitchen, so we descended to the lower regions.

'But Gus,' I asked him in alarm, 'what are you going to cook?

Above: One of my
father Dick
Wyndham's famous
boozy house-parties
at Tickerage Mill.
Left to right: Patrick
Kinross, Constant
Lambert, my father,
Tom Driberg, Cyril
Connolly, part of
Stephen Spender

Right: My aunt
Olivia Wyndham, by
Oliver Messel, before
she ran away to
Harlem

Left: My first husband, the writer Maurice Rowdon

Below: A picnic at Babylon during my stay in Iraq. Khalid Naji, Clare, Rosemary Boxer, self

Wedding Parties
Above: My first wedding party, a very jolly affair in Garratt Lane,
Wandsworth. My new father-in-law (*second left*), my mother-in-law
(*second right*)

Right: Another very festive occasion – Russian this time – after my
wedding to Shura. (Someone has just thrown some red wine over me.)

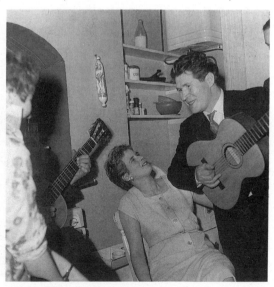

Above left: With Shura, New Year's Eve, 1959

Above right: My eldest daughter Clare

Right: 'Let's Twist Again' has hit the charts, but my younger daughter Camilla and I don't seem to have quite got the hang of it yet

Left: An occasion for celebration! My mother's new companion, Rosamund, finally moves into the cottage

Below right: John – 'mad, bad and dangerous to know'

Below left: With Speedy in Ibiza

Above: Camilla

Right: Sal

Above: With April
Ashley, my co-worker
from the 'Gasworks'
days

Right: New Year's Eve
with Sue and Jonathan
Guinness. A last knees-
up before going into
Westminster Hospital

Joan

This is a proper restaurant, you know – you can't just give them the old spag bol routine.'

'Don't you worry, girl, I've learnt a lot of new tricks since La Roma! It's a doddle, honestly. All you do is get in a lot of frozen chickens and frozen steaks and give them fancy names. Like Lyonnaise, that's with onions, Dijonaise, whack on the mustard, Tangier gets orange slices, Bordelaise, slosh on the red plonk, Swiss means cheese, pineapple means Hawaiian. Jardinière's a good one too,' he went on enthusiastically, 'you can use up all your old leftover vegetables!'

'It sounds easy enough,' I said dubiously. 'Do you think I can manage such a long menu?'

'Nothing to it!' Gus said scornfully. 'The sauces and garnishes and stuff are done ahead – all you do is fry a steak or heat up a piece of chicken and slosh it on!'

I took the menu from him and scanned it carefully. 'Yes, it does seem quite easy – but what's Poussin Gustav's Surprise?'

Gus shook with fiendish laughter. 'That's the easiest of the lot, girl – any old thing in the fridge that you want to get rid of!'

I decided to give it a go, but three weeks later, much to the relief of all concerned, Gus burned the kitchen down, thus giving Bill's customers a happy reprieve.

After Etcetera closed – it was obvious we were not going to make our fortunes – I felt it was time that I packed in the alternative catering caper. But there was one last adventure to come which finally made up my mind for me. I had agreed to work in a small café on the King's Road called Salter's. I arrived to find the owner – a yoga enthusiast – standing on his head by the cash desk. Kids from the Holland Park Comprehensive School dressed up as waiters were darting from table to table, most of them high as kites. I was still trying to get my bearings in a kitchen cubbyhole about three foot by four when a delinquent-looking youth dashed in with an order in one hand and a joint in the other.

'Wanna shot-gun, lady?' he demanded, slamming down an order for two bacon and eggs and taking a drag on his joint.

Before I could ask what a shot-gun was he had clamped his lips firmly over mine and shot a jet of hot acrid smoke straight into my lungs. I broke out into a cold sweat, the kitchen spun around, and I just made it to the cloakroom in time where I collapsed on a pile of coats.

In spite of several brave tries I had always been hopeless with drugs. Pot made me feel ill, cocaine made my nose itch and the thought of acid terrified me – but this was before my trip to Ibiza.

Chapter Eight

Ibiza had always been Shura's territory. He had taken
refuge there when I ran off with John, and had since
kept up a rather vague relationship with a girl called Katya.

In July 1973 he was there again. I had been going through a
rather bad patch, and must have been hell to live with. So we
had both agreed that a break would do us good.

After he left I fell into a pit of depression, but then, out of
the blue, a 'phone call came asking me to join him for the rest
of the holiday. He was missing me and he was worried about
me, but it was important that I came *immediately*! If I didn't
appear by a certain date he would assume I wasn't interested
and go off with Katya on her catamaran. I was amazed and
thrilled and rushed off to book the Friday flight to Palma that
linked up with the Ibiza ferry.

The first panic attack hit me at two in the afternoon, when
the plane had been sitting on the tarmac for one and half hours.
Engine trouble, the stewardess said gaily as she pranced around
with the duty-frees. It was now quite certain that I would miss
the Palma–Ibiza connection and the vital rendezvous with my
husband.

As the plane sat on the tarmac and the heat grew fiercer I
felt my heart fluttering with apprehension. I took rapid shallow
breaths through parted lips. My worst nightmares have always
been about time and travel – missing trains and planes, being
late for urgent appointments, stumbling blindly through

stations and airports unable to read the signs. Thank God, I thought, for the duty-free as a warm comforting gulp of whisky released a single tear. Putting up a finger to brush it away I discovered that one of my false eyelashes was missing – the result no doubt of sleeping fully-clothed on the sofa so as not to miss the plane.

A big bearded man in jeans who was sitting across the aisle from me was eyeing me with curiosity, probably wondering why the lady with the wild blonde hair and one eyelash was crying into her whisky.

At Palma airport I sent a telegram to Ibiza: 'No plane, no boat for two days, no hotel rooms, taking to the beaches. Please wait for me, Joan.'

I was having a last despairing talk to an officer at the information desk when I felt a hulking presence behind me. It was the bearded man in jeans.

'Hi there, my name's O'Casey. I noticed you on the plane. Having trouble?'

I explained my predicament and he laughed reassuringly.

'I've managed to get the last hotel room in Palma, if you're interested. Don't worry, it's got two single beds and anyway I've got friends in town I can stay with.'

I looked at his huge comforting bulk, and felt the panic ebbing. When you're drowning you'll cling to anything. Nevertheless, no one could have been more surprised than I was to find myself, three hours later, strapped to a Victorian brass bedstead in the Hotel Paris y Londres, with a crazed-looking O'Casey unbuckling his brass-studded Mexican belt. I could see wild visions of captive princesses, cringing slave girls and evil sultans whirling past his eyeballs like the cherries on a fruit machine. I let out a scream of terror which seemed to stop him in his tracks.

'Wow!' he said in amazement: 'you're really frightened!' He sounded both surprised and pleased. 'Most women,' he went on, 'think it's all a bit of a joke, they're just play-acting – but you're not faking it, are you? You're really frightened of me!'

'Look,' I said, 'I'm desperately miserable, I'm on the edge of a nervous breakdown, and all I want is a friend to talk to, and someone to help me get through the next few days.'

'Fine with me,' said O'Casey, re-buckling his belt. 'Let's go go down to the café and have some chow. This is my first time out of Canada and I've never tried European food.'

I ordered paella, the most exotic thing on the menu, and O'Casey's eyes widened in surprised delight at the whiskery prawns peering out of a mound of yellow rice. 'Oh boy, look' it those lil' old crawdaddies, just like the ones I catch in the creek back home!' His first European meal, his first European woman – he just couldn't get over it. Only the coffee seemed to faze him a little. 'What's the matter with this cawfee?' he said, looking at the grounds suspiciously. 'What are all those itty bitty black things floating around on top – why don't they melt like in reg'lar cawfee!'

After dinner I got his full life story – how he shot a man in Toronto, killed a grizzly with his bare hands, swam the Yukon in winter. Apparently he had two sides to him – one is a backwoodsman complete with Davy Crockett hat and double-sided axe, while the other is O'Casey the genius sculptor who goes to parties in a purple Hamlet shirt and white Faramir cloak and talks about 'ahrt'. He also confessed that he once drank half a pint of turps in mistake for white wine, so half his brain cells have gone missing. Oh boy, I certainly pick 'em!

Meanwhile all my luggage had gone on to Ibiza. I had no make-up, no toothbrush and no clothes apart from a cotton T-shirt, a floral skirt and one half of my bikini. My nerves were still really bad, and I was still sharing a room with O'Casey – not much choice really. Roll on Monday's boat!

Friday, 20 July. Ibiza at last. To my dismay, Shura has gone. According to his friends he never got my telegram and he's off on the catamaran, probably thinking I don't want to join him.

I am clinging like a limpet to O'Casey, who seems my last link with sanity – I just can't bear to be alone. O'Casey is more than willing. 'I know we got off to a bad start, but why don't we hole up for a while and teach each other everything we know about lovin'?' I saw with relief a warm nest of togetherness instead of the black hole that had been looming before me. He seems a nice enough fellow, apart from his obsession with tying up women. For his part he thought I was his dream lady, a kind of sexy earth mother, not realising I was just a broken arm in search of a splint. This is something I have to keep from him at all costs or he will run away. We are staying for a few days with his friends Kate and Dexter, semi-hippie Americans with two awful kids who make Aunt Jemima hash cookies to take on picnics.

O'Casey is bewitched by the human birds of paradise who flit along the seafront here. 'The theatre of life!' he breathes dramatically. 'What are they all doing here?'

'Pulling ass and dropping dope,' says Dexter laconically. Dexter doesn't like O'Casey – he says he smells funky, even though I'd sluiced him under the pump and given him some nice clean jeans of mine to wear. I feel we have already outstayed our welcome, and have found what is known as a studio apartment by the sea at Calle Llonga. 'Wow, a studio!' said O'Casey, picturing a skylight and a grand piano. He was soon disillusioned. 'Gee, what a crummy hole!' He eyed the divan bed with disgust – 'Not a damn thing to tie a woman up to!'

Wednesday, 1 August. I am still having a sort of affair with O'Casey, but not a very satisfactory one. Basically all he is interested in is sado-masochism, which is not my scene at all. 'The trouble with you', he remarked gloomily, 'is that you're a phoney masochist, but I'm a real sadist!' He won't even let me kiss him. If I try, his lips, writhing with distaste, retreat like snakes into the thicket of his beard. Also he has begun to suspect that I am not the serene mother Ceres figure that he first took me for, but a cripple in search of a crutch.

One day when I could stand my misery no longer, I fell on my knees beside his bed and burst into tears. He jumped up as if I'd burned him. 'Don't *do* that, lady! You hurt so much it freaks me out. I can't stand a beggar and I won't help a cripple. I don't want your fucking heart twitching like a cut worm in front of my feet.'

I stood up and went out on to the balcony, clutching the iron rail until my knuckles were white. All I could say was 'I honestly don't think I could *bear* to be alone right now. Let's stay together for a few more days.'

At least I felt sure he'd stay until Saturday because of the bullfight – all his life he'd dreamed of seeing a bullfight. That week it was Linares and Cordobes, two of the very best, and O'Casey was making excited passes with the bedspread.

We roared into town on his Vespa, where he left me, saying he had to buy souvenirs. I was to meet him at the Mar y Sol hotel, half an hour before the fight.

I was there early, but there was no O'Casey. After a quarter of an hour I began to feel a sick apprehension. With five minutes to go I took a taxi to the bullring, hoping he'd be there ahead of me. My eyes swung from Sol to Sombre, checking the myriads of coloured dots that were blurred by my tears, looking in vain for an orange shirt.

Beneath me Linares moved gently up and down on his toes, arching his body towards the bull like a bent bow. It was a tiny domestic bullring, and I could see the bull's eyelashes and the blood pulsing in his wounded shoulder as he bellowed piteously for his lost meadows. Linares sighted along the sword – the bull had only seconds to live. The sword went in and I watched in disbelief as the bull continued to charge the capes, seemingly unaware of the three foot of steel through its lungs. Then it staggered, and the hot dark blood came pouring out on to the sand just below my seat. Did I imagine it, or were the legs still feebly kicking as they cut the ears off? I shut my eyes, fighting down nausea. When I opened them I saw a flash of orange on the other side of the ring. I jumped to my feet, hurtled down the steps and raced for the opposite exit. The crowd was pouring out, but there was no sign of O'Casey. Thinking he might have gone back to the room already I fought my way through and hitched a car ride into Calle Llonga.

The bare room grinned back at me implacably, empty as a skull. Empty cupboards too – everything had gone. You bastard, I thought, you haven't just left me, you've gone off in my best trousers.

Thank God the apartment block had a bar in the basement, but it was practically empty and I felt conspicuous. I thought the barman was looking at me strangely – women on their own are always presumed to be hunting – so I ordered two large vodkas and carried them over to a dark corner. This was partly so that I could get drunk quicker, and partly to convince the barman that I was sitting with a man. I crouched in my lair and downed them both, repeating this manoeuvre three times. Then I went back to the room and sat on the bed. After a few minutes I thought I heard someone at the window and my heart leapt with hope, but it was only the wind trying to dress itself in my curtains.

I went into the bathroom and laid out, on the one hand, a bottle of sleeping pills and, on the other, my make-up, contact lenses and false eye-lashes, plus a bottle of duty-free Arpège. The pile on the right won hands down and half an hour later, when I finally felt that I looked sufficiently alluring, I called a taxi and drove to the Tavern bar in Ibiza town.

The Tavern is run by an old friend of mine from London called Dave, a tall, thin guy with a long nose. He had just got in a new consignment of records from England – 'White Bird' and 'Jesus Christ Superstar' – and was playing the bit where Christ receives the forty-nine lashes at full blast, much to the dismay of his customers.

I was downing my seventh vodka of the evening when the curtains by the door were parted by a slender brown hand, each nail of which was painted in a different pastel colour. The owner of the hand came in, revealing a young boy with dark mournful eyes and a fringe of hennaed hair under a big straw hat wreathed in flowers.

' 'allo,' he said in a strong French accent. 'You are beautiful!'

'I'm desperate,' I said. 'I want to kill myself.'

'Bon,' the boy said with a pleased smile. 'Let us take this bottle out to the rocks and talk about our sorrows.'

We talked and drank till the early hours, sharing our fears, hopes and weaknesses. Pierre was twenty-one, and lived with his domineering mother in Paris. He had lately been lured by heroin – which he called 'smack' or 'cheval' – but was trying to overcome it. He was also totally impotent.

'I try many times,' he confessed. 'I get excited – but eet does not arrive!'

I asked him what his ambitions in life were. What did he want to be? An ecstatic smile spread across his face. 'I want to be a combination of Marilyn Monroe, Mick Jagère and Buddha!' Poor boy, I thought, you've certainly got problems.

'But what do you actually *do*?' I asked.

'I bore myself to death.'

I told him he looked silly in his straw hat, so he tossed it out to sea, where it floated away like the Never Bird's nest in *Peter Pan*. Now I could admire his long hennaed curls and the sad face spoilt only by a mole on his chin. I couldn't face my lonely room, so he took me back to his apartment in the Square of the Fountain.

I lay in bed feeling peaceful, watching Pierre in his yellow silk kimono moving across the room with his slow, loping stride like a young giraffe, a couple of sandalwood joss sticks sticking out of the corners of his mouth. He inserted them deftly into the keyhole of the wardrobe and climbed into bed with me. Nothing 'arrived', for which I was profoundly grateful. What I needed now was a long period of convalescence.

We were woken at dawn by three boys and a girl from Formentera climbing in through the window and crashing out on the floor. Their knapsacks were wreathed in convolvulus flowers, and one of them carried a tame budgerigar on his shoulder. The bird, who had no tail, hopped from body to body pecking at the pink petals. Later I gave them all a good wash and cooked them brown rice for breakfast.

Meanwhile outside our window the town was waking up. Women in long skirts were carrying jugs to the fountain, children were clacking wooden balls together – this year's favourite toy – and the bars were opening with 'Mammy Blue' and 'Brown Sugar' belting out of the jukeboxes.

Wednesday, 15 August. I am now den mother to half the homeless hippies of this island. I feed them on brown rice, peaches and green tea. I have christened Pierre 'Speedy' because he is so slow.

Speedy's friends on the island are a weird lot! They are really grand French Freaks, and they terrify me. They wear robes of scarlet, saffron and peacock blue, paint their faces with iridescent silver frosting, have long rippling hennaed hair and 'Om' tattooed on their foreheads. The old men in the street call out 'Fiesta!' as they pass. They hang out at a finca in the countryside called Strawberry Fields, and take a lot of drugs.

Meanwhile I have made two new friends I like a lot better. I was in the Tavern when I suddenly heard a cheerful Cockney voice. ''ello, stoned freaks, so'oos gonner buy me a boiled egg then?' and in comes a teenager with long blond hair wearing a kind of white nightdress, followed closely by his clone. They are Nige and Mike, the terrible twins from Hackney, two nice East End kids who have flipped out on Ibiza. Their conversation is minimal:

'Scored a nice bit of Afghani, Mike!'

'Far fuckin' out, Nige!'

Their main purpose in life seems to be to get stoned out of their crusts. They squat like white doves in the corner of our living-room, smoking pot in chillom pipes which they improvise from almost anything, including carrots. Nige is reading *The Lord of the Rings* and keeps us up-to-date on the plot. 'Like Faramir has got it together with his old lady and they've all split for the castle, man!'

The whole town is riddled with drugs – people seem to talk of nothing else. Apart from the usual ones there are Dormedinos, which are sleeping pills, and a cough mixture called Romilar, a kind of hallucinogen. Both are obtainable from the chemist, who must be wondering why all the foreigners on Ibiza are insomniacs with laryngitis. I am worried about Speedy. Every now and then he gets terribly restless and makes some excuse to leave the house. As I watch from the window his long, loping stride suddenly turns into a run, and he throws back his head and kicks up his heels ecstatically like a young ram in springtime before disappearing in the direction of the port. When he comes back he seems much calmer and happier and starts unscrewing the main light fixtures – a well-known place, apparently, for junkies to hide their goodies. He says he is changing the bulbs, but I know better as none of the lights work and we live by candlelight. In fact, I think I know who Speedy's pusher is – a drug addict called Pauline, who is super-smart and super-nasty, as only the Parisian French can be. She has the sort of habit that has to be fed every four hours like a baby. No tattered jeans or saffron robes for her – she wears Dior linen sun-suits with a straw hat that comes down over her ears like a helmet. I hate her, and she hates me.

When I had it out with her, and told her to lay off Speedy, she replied icily, 'Tu me fais chier, ma chère.' How dare she be so cool and self-confident with no veins left?

As for me, I smoke a bit, but the whole drug scene bores me stiff. I'm so happy that I don't need them. For the last few weeks I have felt totally peaceful, with not a twinge of fear, anxiety or guilt. I live entirely in the present, unmindful of the past and unafraid of the future – something I have always longed for but never managed to achieve till now. In this fantasy island, totally divorced from reality, my mind is a blank, resting itself. I haven't read a single line of a book or newspaper, or heard a telephone ring, but I listen to music a great deal. As for the beach, I think I've only seen it once since I arrived.

I have written about all this to Shura, now back at work in London, and he says he understands. I think he realises this escapade is harmless – a sort of *safe* version of the 'John' episode – and that I need to 'get my head together', as the Terrible Twins would say. In fact I think he's quite relieved to be rid of me for a while.

Wednesday, 22 August. I have been in Ibiza now for nearly four weeks. I love Speedy and he loves me, but in a very pure way because 'nothing arrives'. Not that I wouldn't like it to – I try to tell myself that he is a brother or a son figure, but who am I fooling? I long to touch him but I dare not. I long to stroke his thin, unmuscled arms, like those of a young girl in her first ball gown, but he flinches from any touch. We still sleep together, but there's only the occasional friendly hug. In order to explain to his smart friends his rather extraordinary relationship with a fifty-year-old woman he has put it about that I am a very wealthy lady and that he is my gigolo.

'It is vairy, vairy important that you should be *extremely* rich!' he explains to me. He loves to tease me by prancing up and down in front of my café table singing 'I'm just a gigolo'. Thought for the day (via Neil Young and the Terrible Twins)

'Is it hard to make arrangements with yourself
When you're old enough to repaint
But young enough to sell?'

The only snag is that I'm not rich at all, in fact I'm down to my last seventy quid and everyone seems to expect me to pay for their meals.

Sunday, 26 August. For days now Speedy has talked of nothing but visiting Didi, his old friend and guru, who has arrived on the neighbouring island of Formantera. He is about twelve years older than Speedy and sounds like a nasty piece of work to me, but Speedy is obviously under his spell. It was Didi who first turned him onto drugs.

On the boat to Formentera the sky turned green at midday and I felt it was a bad sign. The island is even more drug-obsessed than Ibiza – the hippies and dealers squat around the main square in full daylight peddling their wares and weighing out dubious substances on little scales. I saw Speedy buy something and slip it in his pocket.

We went into a huge café with a dance floor and ordered a coffee. Suddenly there was a scream of pleasure and a creature in a black mini-skirt and a straw hat came running towards us across the huge floor. As he ran a budgie with no tail took off from his hat and fluttered ahead of him, landing back on the brim as he fell on Speedy's neck. It was Didi.

On the long trek back to his house in the hills we spotted the glint of empty Romilar bottles gleaming in the sand, like magic signals leading to the ogre's castle.

Spent an extremely tedious evening listening to Didi playing his new toy, Tibetan bells. Even Speedy looked a bit pissed-off.

Later I was put to bed in a hammock in the same room as Didi's wife and child, a delicious little girl called Isis-Colombe. Through a lighted doorway I could see Didi sitting at a table with a syringe on it, carefully heating a spoon over a candle flame.

The wind brought the sound of drums and flutes from the Blue Bar on the beach. There was no sign of Speedy but he woke me at dawn and we fled back to Ibiza.

Wednesday, 29 August. Disaster has struck. Didi turned up from Formantera, dressed like a medieval page, with a sleeping child in his arms. Apparently he has left his wife, Esmerelda, who he says is a bitch and a whore, kidnapped the baby, and intends to move in with Speedy. I, apparently, will be looking after Isis-Colombe! *Groovy!* Here we are on this siren's isle, with everybody dancing, making love and getting high, and I am stuck with a grubby, tearful two-year-old.

So, here's the new set-up. Didi and Speedy in one bed, me and Isis-Colombe in the other. She cries for her mother in the night, poor little sausage, and I try to comfort her with sweets.

Speedy and Didi seem to spend most of the daylight hours in bed, like two vampires, only surfacing when it gets dark. Didi takes a tablet out of his leather pouch and pops it like a holy wafer into Speedy's open fledgling mouth.

'Zoom, zoom!' he says, and they run off together spreading their arms out and flying into the night like bats.

Friday, 7 September. A week has gone by, and I still haven't managed to get rid of Didi and the baby. Nige and Mike don't come to the house any more – it's no longer their scene. Anyone who peddles hard drugs is anathema to them. Nigel is having an affair with a really heavy chick called Tania who gives him a great ego buzz, or so he tells me. Mike, on the other hand, spends a lot of time in chemists' shops and is permanently out of his bonce on something or other.

Didi keeps trying to butter me up. He calls me 'Diamant' and has bought me a beautiful Ibizincan peasant skirt in faded pink cotton. But Speedy, who is basically a fairly sophisticated person, is beginning to see through him and to find him *boring* – the most damning word in his vocabulary. He is fed up with his paranoia, his childlike tears and tantrums. Most of all he hates him because Didi wants him back on heroin.

One night there was a final explosive scene and Didi finally left, driven out by blows from Speedy's fist and cries of 'ordure!' – an extraordinary display of violence from such a gentle creature, but Speedy had had his fill of this little monster. Didi and the child are now back with Esmerelda and we are at peace again.

* *

Sunday, 9 September. Today, drinking jasmine tea at the Bar Chichi, Speedy says for the first time 'I love you' – I told him I loved him too. 'You understand,' he went on, 'this is not just for now but for eternity.'

On the way back to the house he took my hand and said 'Will you drop acid with me tomorrow?' I felt terrified but at the same time immensely excited. Then common sense took over. You don't start on acid at my age, I told myself, and went to ask Dave at the Tavern for his advice.

'Listen, lady,' said good old down-to-earth Dave, 'I'm going to lay a heavy rap on you. You are a fifty-year-old woman temporarily knocked off your feet by the simultaneous discovery of rock music, pot and young boys, and frankly I think it's doing your head in. Why don't you sober up, act your age and get your karma together! However if you do decide to be an idiot and drop acid, take my advice and don't look in the mirror!'

We swallowed it sitting at a café table in the morning sunshine, down by the old port. It looked like a piece of blotting paper with two transparent drops on it. Obediently I swallowed one half, and Speedy took the other.

Did I expect an instant revelation? Nothing happened. I had a cigarette, drank a Fanta and we hitched a ride to the nude beach at the end of Salinas, a private place where freaks go to wash out their robes and scrub themselves in the sea with sand. Still nothing was happening, so I stripped off and went for a swim. As I paddled back towards the beach I saw Speedy sitting by the edge of the water, holding in his hand a playing card which the sea had washed up. Except – somehow – it wasn't Speedy any more. Crouching down on the sand beside him, I looked up into his face and saw it begin to shift and change. The sun was still shining, the sand was firm and damp to the touch, but Speedy was metamorphosing into a devil, an angel and finally a woman with a face of radiant beauty like the moon goddess who rules over Ibiza. Then slowly his face began to melt into long blue waxen tears, his eyes burning like red candles in their empty sockets. I could see the green phosphorescent bones glowing through his yellow robes.

When I told him what I was seeing he just laughed at me. He is an old hand at this game and never hallucinates. 'You're tripping too heavily,' he said, almost enviously, and I saw the mocking laughter shoot out of his mouth like a long black flickering tongue that hissed at me.

I ran away as fast as I could and soon found a nice large rock behind which I could hallucinate in peace. For the next three hours – though it was probably only minutes – I went on a long and glorious exploration of outer space. I came back to earth with a bump to find a rather intense-looking American girl trying to catch my attention.

'Hi,' she chirped with a winning smile, 'you haven't by any chance got a nail-file?'

I gazed at her in disbelief. 'Listen, lady, I've just been three times round the universe, dropped in on Mars and Venus, skidded down the Milky Way and visited Betelgeuse by way of Alpha Centuri. The man on the rock over there has just turned into a crocodile, my big toe is sprouting a potato and you want to know if I've got a NAIL-FILE?'

The unfortunate girl withdrew crestfallen and I went back to contemplating my big toe, which was now growing roots.

Later I went for a walk through the 'straight' beach, feeling intense paranoia, like an alien fallen to earth. Surely they could see that I looked totally different? There were packs of wild Ibizincan dogs running along the beach beside me, golden sparks flying from their nostrils. Animals look great on acid, humans less so as they tend to mutate into the animal they most resemble – not always a pleasant sight. The bodies sunbathing on the beach looked like roasting pigs.

Back at the house we cooked spaghetti, and it was fun watching it try to crawl out of the pot. But even when you're tripping you have to go to the loo, and while I was in the bathroom I decided to check out my appearance and see if I looked as odd as I felt. I'd forgotten Dave's warning not to look in the mirror, but by now it was too late.

I could see my face getting younger by the second, the dark shadows chasing each other from under my eyes, wrinkles fading, chin firming and eyes brightening as I raced back towards childhood and the cradle. I was just about to be sucked back into the womb when the tape changed direction and started a furious fast-forward towards old age and death. Terrified, I tried to hold the frame rigid at the flawless face of eighteen, but it began to quiver and dissolve, slipping away from me down the corridors of time, the flesh drying and wrinkling, hair greying, heading for decomposition and the tomb.

Fearing that any second I'd be a heap of ashes on the bathroom floor I grasped the flesh of my cheekbones with both hands, moulding the mask of fifty back into place, and flinging myself away from the mirror and onto the floor.

As I came back into the bedroom, sobbing with exhaustion, I found Speedy on the bed, his arms outstretched towards me. The brown bedspread that lay over him crawled like a snake trying to shed its skin.

'I am having a truth trip,' he said, 'and I want you to look at me closely. I am not an angel or a devil or a moon goddess, but I went along with all that nonsense because I knew it gave you pleasure. Look closely – I am not really so handsome, I am rather an ugly little boy with a mole on my chin, and you are a woman obsessed with growing old. What are you afraid of? Don't you know how inspired young men are by older women, what a powerful strength you have? Just never let it crumble, never show weakness. I want you as a kind of mother goddess, and it frightens me when you show fear.'

He picked up my hand and kissed it. 'Shall we make love now, or shall we go first and dance at Lola's?'

I knew perfectly well that we would do neither of these things – and I was dead right, for a few minutes later Speedy said, quite sweetly, 'And now would you please do me the infinite favour of leaving me to myself,' and fell deeply asleep, with no hope of being woken.

I felt suddenly panic-stricken. On your first trip it is important to be with someone whom you love and trust, someone to communicate with, and now I was alone with this great tearing energy raging through my heart and my sex. To make things even more dramatic, an electric storm had broken out.

I did the only thing possible: I lined up scouring-powder and brushes and pails of water and started cleaning the flat. I even scrubbed out the shower and the loo. There was a tremendous flash of lightning and all the lights went out. Terrified, I crawled on all fours looking for sleeping pills, anything to bring me down. Finally I found a bottle of Dormadinos, swallowed a handful and mercifully passed out.

Thursday, 20 September. A letter arrived from London which brought me down to earth with a bump. Cammy, who has been working at the Bush Theatre, is coming here for a well-deserved holiday. She probably thinks I'm still with Ann and Dexter, having a jolly time on the beach – ha ha. The time has finally come for me to clean up my act. I can't say I regret the last two months – they've been amazing. I've drunk from every stream, even those marked poisonous, sniffed every flower, tested the edge of every blade, stroked the horn of the unicorn. Now it's time to come back to a bit of normality! Speedy, thank God, seems to be off the heroin.

The first thing to do is to move out of the house in Ibiza and take a small bungalow in the woods near Santa Eulalia. Something nice and quiet and healthy! I said a sad farewell to our room. The burnt-out ends of sandalwood joss-sticks stuck like porcupine quills from every orifice, and their soft grey ash lay inches deep on the floor.

I took the sheets to the launderette and cleaned out the whole place thoroughly, sweeping up enough grass from the floor to stone half Ibiza. I also found my missing contact lens in the process. In spite of all this, the uptight French lady who finally rented it from us took one look at the place and said 'Eet ees a peeg-sty!' Silly bitch. She should have seen it last week!

The second thing was to hire a car – a clapped out old Citroen – for trips to the beach, which I've hardly seen for two months except under rather curious circumstances.

The third thing was to make sure that the more unsavoury elements in Ibiza town don't know our new address. Luckily Pauline is no longer a menace as she was busted last week and is now doing cold turkey chained by her wrists and ankles to a bed in the prison hospital.

Tuesday, 25 September. Cammy arrived at the airport looking all chirpy and expectant in a Fifties dress with huge blue and white polka dots and a big straw hat.

She and Speedy clicked immediately and soon were going everywhere together. If they were lambs they would be gambolling. I no longer feel like a sophisticated older woman with a young gigolo, more like some old maiden aunt in charge of two naughty children.

Cammy approved of the bungalow among the pine woods but took one look at the brown rice cooking in the kitchen and said in dismay 'Oh Christ, mother's gone macro-biotic!' I felt so guilty that I took them both out for an enormous meal – steak Bèarnaise and Crêpes Suzette. It cost a bomb.

Cammy seems totally unfazed by the fact that Speedy wears weird clothes and glitter on his cheekbones, but is firmly bent on stamping out any signs of hippiness in *me*! Watching her unpack her duty-free Silk Cut I asked, unthinkingly, for 'a straight'. 'What do you mean, a *straight*, Mummy? Why can't you say "cigarette?" I suppose it'll be "far out" and "right on" next! And you, with your marvellous vocabulary!' I can see I'm going to have to watch my step, though I still smoke the occasional joint and have learnt to like it – that wonderful cool, stoned feeling when the river of time stops flowing.

I haven't much money left, so we live mainly on vegetable soup, pancakes and cheap white wine and play endless records. Our favourites are Santana Abraxa, Elton John's black album (the one with 'Your Song' on it), Neil Young's 'After the Goldrush', and Cat Stevens's 'Tea for the Tillerman'. We sleep well and peacefully, lulled by the cicadas, stupefied by the scent of the pines, and nothing 'arrives' in any direction.

So far only one of our old friends has managed to track us down, a blond mophead in a white robe carrying a homemade bamboo water pipe – it was Nige. 'Hi man, mind if I drop in for a quick schmoodle? My old lady Tania has just blown me out and I'm on this raging bummer. I suppose I couldn't crash out here?'

'No, you couldn't,' I said firmly.

'So how 'bout laying a little bread on me then? Our mum hasn't sent any for ages.'

No again.

'That's cool, man.' Not in the least upset, Nige settled down happily in a corner with his water pipe for a schmoodle.

In the evening we all went to Lola's Club and danced like maniacs. Now that Cammy's here we are doing a lot more dancing, and I love it. I find that when I'm moving to music I can forget myself completely, which is what I like best. Speedy is a dreadful dancer, so Cammy and I gyrate on our own, using Lola's as a kind of gym.

* *

Friday, 28 September. Great excitement – the British battle-ship *Penelope* has arrived in the harbour. Cammy came rushing in to say that she had made friends with a sailor and we are all invited aboard. Speedy, who was wearing one of Cammy's Twenties dresses in flowered chiffon, leapt into action – he has always been mad about sailors – and changed into a nice clean T-shirt and white trousers. After that he rather spoilt the effect by spending an hour on his make-up.

Off we went to get pissed in the officers' wardroom. Speedy tried gamely to talk to the captain about torpedoes and so on and everything was going swimmingly, when the captain, handing Speedy a vodka and lime, suddenly freaked out on his mandarin-length fingernails, glistening with Cammy's Mary Quant Frosted Grape. He soon rallied like a true British officer, but we could hear him hiss in the first mate's ear 'I say, old chap, don't look now but I think that French bounder's wearing nail varnish!'

Sunday, 30 September. Today I did a rather shameful thing. I can never resist other people's diaries – if they don't want them read they shouldn't leave them lying about. (I am very careful with mine!)

Speedy had been writing in Cammy's diary all morning, and when they went out to buy Fanta I couldn't resist taking a peep. To my annoyance he had written in French and his handwriting was appalling, but one phrase leapt out of the page and hit me. 'Je meure de l'amour!' – 'I am dying of love!' Turning back to the beginning I was able to translate a few phrases.

So here we are again, three people in one room. It's not too bad – one can put up with it for a little while. At least we are not bored, though sometimes I feel the urge to scream 'Je m'emmerde!' – but I am not built for action or for changing things. I suppose I could always drug myself – but no! I feel a frisson of terror at the very thought. Brrr. Now it passes and I breathe more easily.

I die of love! Douce et belle, sweet and beautiful like some amazing flower that one sees at evening beside a stream, under the shelter of a tree. You are dangerous, *ma belle*, and I feel myself already lost, like a child astonished in front of the beauty of a new toy. My mouth hangs open and my arms dangle. I no longer know what to do with my life and I drown in a passion which rends my heart and my eyes, leaving me wounded and unsatisfied.

For about five seconds I actually thought that he was writing about me. What presumption! Turning back the pages to Camilla's own diary I saw that she had written 'I am a little in love with Speedy but I won't trouble them with it, I don't want to spoil things for Mummy. He and I are lost children inhabiting the same limbo, not knowing where or who to turn to. In five days they go back – I shall miss them both so much.' Before I could read any more I heard them coming back through the pine trees with their arms full of branches for the fire, laughing and singing. As they were making the fire next door they were talking about me, and I heard Cammy's bell-like tones saying 'I suppose she thinks of you as a girl.' Unfortunately I don't – in fact I am horribly and humiliatingly jealous, which I know is ridiculous, but I can't help it.

There is only one thing to do: forget what I have read, forget who loves whom, and make the most of our last few days together. Speedy and I will be travelling back to Paris soon, but Cammy has elected to stay on in Ibiza for another week. Speedy is furious and thinks unjustly that I've engineered their parting – but this is not true.

Monday, 1 October. Full moon in Ibiza, an island dedicated to the moon goddess. A time when wild parties are held and murderers get off scot-free. But tonight is something special – not just a full moon, but a full moon in eclipse! We are celebrating at Strawberry Fields, the craziest finca on the island.

The huge courtyard was lit by flares, and by children who ran around like fireflies waving torches. All around were black-bearded freaks banging away on African drums and Tibetan bells, while in the centre of the square the rich French poseurs gyrated slowly in their ethnic robes.

Suddenly my daughter could stand it no longer and leapt to her feet. She looked crisp, cool and sharp as a knife in her white Forties dress, picked up in some King's Road nostalgia shop, tight red belt, flaring skirt, Minnie Mouse shoes with high high heels, plastic beads and a red bow on the top of her head. Without more ado she dragged Speedy into the throng and went into a fast jive. Everyone gaped at her, but I cheered and started to bang out a fast rhythm on a drum with my sandals. Spotting a long pipe sticking out into the sea, she began to prance along it as if it were a cat-walk, fingers clicking, full skirt whipping round her legs, a white moth under the hazy moon which was fast going into eclipse. Speedy couldn't take his eyes off her.

Thursday, 4 October. Speedy and I finally left on the night boat to Barcelona. All the French hippies turned up on the quayside with drums and flutes to see us off. Speedy, already drunk, watched Cammy's figure dwindling as the boat pulled out. As the last streamer parted he up-ended his vodka bottle and poured the rest of it down his throat.

I thought Cammy would be glad to see the last of us, but it was not so. She wrote in her diary: 'O.K., so they've gone now, so drunk that I had to practically carry them on to the boat. They looked very happy. They said it would be good for me to be independent, and all the young men would be dying to take me out to dinner. But I feel soaked in sober melancholic gloom, I miss them so much. In their company, for one short month I felt pretty, sexy and intelligent, and now I'm back to being my former enclosed self.'

Saturday, 6 October. En route to Paris we are stopping off at La Rose Rouge which belongs to a rich hippy called Tristram. I had visions of French country cooking, bidets, washing-machines and ironing-boards – in fact all the accoutrements of civilised living. Imagine my dismay when we arrived to find yet another hippy commune, with flutes and bongos, brown rice, mattresses on the floor, Ravi Shankar and peeing in the bushes.

Tristram has long red hair down to his waist and wears pale blue, diamond-shaped glasses and a saffron robe. Put him in normal gear, give him a haircut and horn-rims and he'd look like a successful banker. Instead he plays the flute, and acts as host to a motley crew who like to walk around naked, getting stoned, and occasionally sally out to rip off some fruit and veg from the local farmer.

We sleep on filthy mattresses in a big communal room, recently vacated by the Rainbow Gypsies, an esoteric dance troupe who have left behind a smell of sweat and sandalwood. They are not very popular with the commune as they stole all the blankets and gave clap to half the commune.

Occasionally Speedy takes Tristram aside and I can hear the words 'extrèmement riche' and 'cinquante ans' – I'm getting extremely bored with this scenario, especially as I'm broke.

Upstairs is the domain of Tristram's friend Marie-France, an amazingly beautiful transsexual cabaret artiste from Paris who has real breasts and wears full evening dress all the time. We followed the whirring of a sewing-machine and found her treadling away at yards and yards of heavy grey satin for another ball gown.

'I suppose you haven't got any booze?' she asked hopefully in a deep bass voice.

'Only crème de menthe,' I said apologetically.

'Fantastique, cherie, bring up some ice and we'll make frappés'.

I could see Speedy was riveted by her and I could see why. She looked exactly like Didi in drag.

At sunset they both disappeared for hours. Looking out over the aromatic bushes spread with drying rags of purple and saffron I could see two tiny figures, one yellow, one black, walking side by side so close that they could have been holding hands.

So now I am alone again, bored and paranoid. Speedy and Marie-France talk of nothing but Paris. He's also been getting letters in a strange green spidery hand writing which seem to excite him strangely. 'They are from Katya Krishna! She is a vairee, vairee beautiful innocent girl, one of the purest souls I ever met!' I hate her already.

To make matters worse, Ninette, the bitchy queen of the commune, has taken a dislike to me. I creep around in terror of her in my bare feet and long pink skirt, walking with small steps, my eyes cast down like some nervous postulant, a new novice among old initiates.

Sometimes I go into town and see a film on my own. Last night it was Mick Jagger in *Gimme Shelter*, with very funny subtitles. When Jagger snarls 'Like, cool it man, you're fucking up my trip!' it comes out as 'Du calme, mon gars, tout est vraiment tres désagréable!'

On other nights I work in the kitchen, slipping Maggi cubes into their veggie stew. They just can't get over how good it tastes. I also got the whole commune pissed by giving them rough cider from the farm and telling them it was pure organic apple juice. I had never seen freaks so happy, but Ninette was furious. I feel it's time for us to move on.

Wednesday, 10 October. Left the Rose Rouge in a caravan of hippy buses, rolling down the Route Nationale 6 towards Paris. These vans are fantastic, fitted with mattresses, oriental carpets and water pipes. Green tea bubbles merrily on the stove and Ravi Shankar wails from the stereo speaker. We sleep four to a mattress and live on goats' cheese and stolen grapes. Today Speedy and I went into a shop to buy some paté. 'Bonjour, mes dames!' said the nice old biddy behind the counter who had only seen Speedy's top half with its long hennaed curls.

Twenty miles out of Paris there was a sudden dive behind the bed curtains. Robes were thrown aside, hair was clipped and make-up scrubbed off as Speedy and his friends struggled back into grey flannel trousers, clean white shirts and imitation Shetland pullovers, ready to be reunited with Papa et Maman.

Speedy's Maman is quite terrifying. She has cropped reddish hair, beige stockings and a very short kilt, and looks like an old-style Resistance fighter. She lives alone ten flights up in an almost totally bare flat furnished with camping chairs and a primus stove. It was obvious she hated me on sight. 'Why is your mother so unpleasant?' I asked. 'Because I am her only son and she is like an old fierce tigress protecting me from other women.' Needless to say the only female she tolerates is that boring creep Katya Krishna, the one who is so terribly pure and spiritual, and works in a macro-biotic café called the Wooden Bowl.

Paris gives me the creeps. The girls are all so closed and up-tight and the men so serious. I try very hard to be friendly and to give a good impression but without much success.

Speedy says they think I must be a whore because they're not used to women being frank and open. This came as a great disappointment as I had hoped at least to be taken for a Swedish filmstar.

Sunday, 14 October. I have finally met the dreaded Katya Krishna. She wears a sort of burnt orange cloak with a hood, has shining pink cheeks without make-up and is totally humourless. When she saw me she made a great pretence of being shy and embarrassed and finally ran away as if I had the plague. Odious child!

Speedy, who has not yet been able to scrounge any money from his parents, is still treating me like a rich patroness. 'Pay, pay!' he snarled at me in a cake shop today while I fumbled with my purse: 'you know how to pay, don't you?' He keeps hinting that other women in the past have given him 'little presents'. If we go into a bar he always orders a Brandy Alexander, because he says it is the most boring and expensive drink that he knows. Why is he doing this? Is he trying to get rid of me so that he can spend more time with Katya Krishna? Thank God there's only a few more days to go. As for Cammy, he has never mentioned her once since we left Ibiza.

Wednesday, 17 October. My last day. Maman very charming to me. 'Why is your mother being so nice to me, Speedy?' 'Because you are leaving.'

Lunch at the Wooden Bowl, with Katya Krishna looking smug behind the bar. She gave us two bowls and some chopsticks and served us with some totally unseasoned millet garnished with seaweed – revolting! I was hoping that after lunch we could go back to the hotel and spend a quiet evening talking and drinking for the last time, but Katya soon put a stop to that by slipping Speedy a mescalin trip hidden in a tube of organic toothpaste.

By the time we hit the Deux Magots, Speedy was already flying. There is nothing more boring than somebody else's trip when you're straight yourself.

I saw him muttering to a huge Negro in a purple jumpsuit, and soon we were speeding off in the direction of Orly airport in the Negro's enormous chauffeur-driven Cadillac. He is called 'Explosion' because this is what he shouts in moments of passion.

We parked among the trees just near the runway, and the chauffeur spread a big sheet of bright blue plastic on the grass. We lay down side by side, while the chauffeur in peaked cap and black mirrored glasses leant nonchalantly against the bonnet.

As the first Caravelle roared over our heads, the Negro gave a great shout of 'Explosion!' and leapt on me from behind. I discouraged him with a sharp kick and clung to Speedy, who suddenly and unexpectedly gave me the most angelic smile, and began to kiss me. Not little boys' kisses, but proper ones, hugging me and stroking my neck and shoulders. I was happy for the first time since we'd come to Paris.

We escaped as soon as we could and raced back to the hotel, where we changed into our most glamorous clothes and went dancing.

About three in the morning back in my hotel bedroom, I woke to see a tall figure in a yellow silk kimono standing beside my bed. 'I theenk eet has arrived!' Speedy said happily – and it had. It was very sweet, very gentle, like the wings of a moth brushing against your cheek in the night.

When we woke he took the glass beads from his wrist and hooked them round mine. They were turquoise and purple, the colours of grapes and the sea. Then he gave me his most beautiful smile and said 'I think it has been very good for me to know you.'

At the airport he was charming and attentive, but something stirred in my memory. 'Why is your mother being so nice to me?' 'Because you are leaving.'

On the plane I cried and drank whisky as usual. Why is it I'm always sitting in aeroplanes drunk and with tears streaming down my face when everybody else is sitting bolt upright reading *The Times* and eating tinned fruit salad from plastic dishes?

As soon as I got home I wrote him a letter, a lot of corny nonsense about how much he had taught me that I would never forget and how we were friends for life. I urged him to come over and stay with us in London – just as friends, no strings attached – and though I tried to sound cool and detached, I ended up flooding the page with tenderness and nostalgia. I even used the most shameful ploy of all – 'Cammy sends her love and is longing to see you again.'

Ten days later my letter was returned. On it, in a familiar hand in spidery green ink, was written 'Inconnu. N'existe pas. N'habite pas içi.'

I never saw or heard from Speedy again.

Chapter Nine

N I had now reached the end of my life as a middle-aged hippie. Slowly but surely I got rid of my kaftans to jumble sales, and went in for smart little numbers from the Harvey Nichols' half-price sales. Certain records could still reduce me to tears, but on the whole I had returned to normality and also to a much more stable relationship with Shura.

I think it was my idea that we should go to Russia. For years now Shura had been playing gypsy music, leaping in the air and landing on one knee (often with disastrous consequences) and generally wallowing in his nostalgia for the old country. Now I thought it was time he found out what it was really like.

Needless to say we did nothing as normal as taking an aeroplane. Instead we boarded a bus for Leningrad at Kings Cross Station and travelled overland through Copenhagen, where I saw my first blue film, and Finland, where everybody seemed to be drunk by six o'clock in the evening.

On our last night before Russia, we boarded a Swedish boat and stuffed ourselves on the most wonderful buffet, like camels filling our humps before the gastronomic desert of Russia – quite rightly, as things turned out.

In the early morning we glided in through an archipelago of tiny islands, and got for the first time the real feeling of being 'altogether elsewhere'. Soon we were in the woods with signs saying 'Beware of Moose'. 'Bush stop,' bellowed our Australian driver. 'Everybody out, no more doings before Russia!' and we bolted for the birch trees.

Soon the Russian frontier loomed up, complete with sinister-looking watch towers. 'There it is,' said our driver gloomily, 'just like on the movies! We'll probably be here for hours. But don't worry, you won't be bored – there'll be something happening every minute. Something nasty!'

Meanwhile Russian officials were positioning our coach over a pit so that officials could climb down and examine its bottom for people mad enough to try and enter Russia illegally.

By the time we reached baggage inspection, Shura was feeling distinctly paranoid, since his wallet was stuffed with the addresses of dissident friends. After rejecting the idea of swallowing them, he went to the loo to flush them down, only to find it had no doors – presumably in case you tried to top yourself to escape arrest.

Two hours later we were free, and heading in the rain for Viborg and our first Russian meal. It was served in a vast, gloomy restaurant over the railway station, which seemed to be filled with crowds supplied by Moscow Central Casting, like being back in some very old, silent revolutionary movie. Old peasant ladies in shawls and felt boots, carrying their luggage in tin pails, plodded past with their hugely pregnant daughters, a surly uniformed official knocked the cigarette out of my hand, gypsies in broad-brimmed hats drank from bottles, and Mongols and Tartars fixed us with their squinting eyes.

I asked for the loo, and a babushka escorted me to a filthy tiled room with loos on one side, urinals on the other, and one toilet roll stuck to the wall on a nail. There were also several nasty plastic containers in which to deposit your used paper or old sanitary towels. An ancient crone of unsavoury appearance was engaged in slurping brown scum from one side of the floor to the other with the aid of her husband's old grey underpants on the end of a long stick.

Then came lunch in a room with marble pillars and chandeliers, served on battered silver by slatterns in tight black skirts with lots of eye make-up, their blonde beehives in considerable disarray.

We had some oily smoked fish, a sinister soup made from cabbage and chickens' arseholes, and a piece of rock-hard gristly beef on a mound of grey, boiled potatoes. As we left we noticed to our dismay that the waitresses were removing all the pieces of uneaten meat, and piling them up in a separate pot, presumably for tomorrow's meatballs!

What we didn't realise was that this identical meal would be served to us every day, twice a day, throughout our stay in Russia.

Monday, 4 August 1975. We reached Leningrad at dusk – the most beautiful city in Russia, with its pale gold, white and blue Italianate palaces on the banks of the Neva.

We are staying in the suburbs in a modern hotel set in a park. As we sat in the vast restaurant toying with our gristle and spuds, the band tore into a jazz version of 'Tea for Two' and everyone took to the floor – fat ladies with their fat daughters, boys in uniform with girls in flowery nylon dresses, and peasants enjoying a night out.

Took the underground into town – everything blindingly white and smelling of disinfectant. There are no bra ads on the escalators, and the couples going down stand facing each other so as not to have to stop talking.

Inside the carriage I felt as if I was on another planet – everything seemed so innocent, so utterly uncontemporary. The girls were still wearing mini-skirts. As it was Air Force Day, a public holiday, everyone was carrying armfuls of gladioli and maidenhair ferns. Peasants were returning with empty vegetable baskets to their farms, drunks were being dragged home by fierce, deep-bosomed wives, and there was much horseplay and kissing.

At Nevski Prospekt the streets were full of stalls selling dumplings, pies, pancakes and icecream, and upstairs, behind lighted windows, we could see the shadows of youngsters jiving.

Tuesday, 5 August. Our first breakfast. We shared our table with a soft, gentle-eyed spinster lady, redolent of lavender, who talked of poetry and Chopin. She turned out to be the foreman of an engineering factory in the Urals.

Breakfast was black bread, sour milk, garlic sausage, tepid

boiled tongue and yellow processed peas. We had to wait forty minutes for a cup of coffee.

The whole coach had been agog to meet our Russian guide, Sergei. We had been warned that he would watch us like a hawk to make sure we didn't make foreign contacts. To our surprise the dreaded agent of the K.G.B. turned out to be a nice blond myopic student with a disarmingly wicked smile.

His tour of Leningrad was perfunctory, ending in the Hermitage, where dazed Russians were shuffling through wall-to-wall Rembrandts carrying baskets of *piroshki* wrapped in copies of *Pravda*.

'Oh look, Kostya,' cried one child to another as they gazed at a picture of St Sebastian pierced with arrows, 'look how they used to kill people in the bad old days before the Revolution!'

Spent the evening watching a terrible folk ballet – there was one extremely embarrassing number where the dancers dressed up as samovars and teacups. Afterwards Sergei came back to our hotel room with us, and he and Shura got terribly pissed and started telling Armenian jokes. Armenian jokes are extremely basic and simple. For instance: 'Tell me, comrade, after uranium bomb will we find toilets?' 'After uranium bomb, comrade, first find your ass!' Or even worse: *Q* What are ten pricks on a rope? *A* The Volga boatmen! It was not a very cultural evening.

Round about midnight we ended up in a bar of the Metropole Hotel where a band called the Red Cats was playing 'Down Mexico Way', and tarts with silver eye make-up and stilettoes lined the bar stools. We were advised to try drinking something called *yersh*.

'What is *yersh*?' asked Sergie: 'a small fish with sharp ends?'

'No,' said the barman, who looked like an eminent brain surgeon, '*yersh* is vodka with beer, and it gets you so drunk that you'll walk out on your eyebrows.'

'Whatever it is, let's have it!' said Sergei happily. 'We Russians like to drink,' he added unnecessarily. 'We have a saying in Russia, "Let's drink till the pulse stops!" '

'But won't you have a hangover tomorrow?' I asked anxiously.

'Nothing that 500 grammes of vodka for breakfast won't cure!'

Just then the Viking Tours contingent arrived from the camp site. The barman put on a much-treasured and scratched record of 1967's Top Ten – pirated from Eastern Europe – and the Vikings took the floor.

'What Western atmosphere!' cried Sergei, moist-eyed with happiness as a Viking yobbo hurled his partner to the floor to the strains of 'A Whiter Shade of Pale'. 'Never would you think you were in Russian bar! Tell me,' he went on, gazing into my eyes, 'what is your favourite pop record? Me, I like very much "Rocky Racoon" by Simon and Garfunkel, and "Brown Sugar" by Beatles!'

Friday, 8 August. Moscow at last! Queued up at the Kremlin where I struck the local gold teeth contingent dumb by sticking the sole of my sandal on with chewing-gum. They beamed with delight, and some even clapped at this display of capitalist ingenuity. The Kremlin treasures are amazing, but I never want to see another onion dome.

Sergei's deterioration continues. When asked if he was going to accompany us to the Exhibition of Economic Achievement he said the Russian equivalent of 'Sod that, comrades, I'm going to sleep off my hangover.' We decided to do the same.

Tonight great excitement – we actually got a chicken rissole! After dinner everyone was packed off to the circus, but we opted out like bad sports and retired to bed. To our surprise there was a knock on the door, and in came Sergei with a bottle of vodka and his entire collection of pop tapes, including the whole of *Tommy* and *Jesus Christ Superstar*. He and Shura got very drunk and recorded forty minutes of non-stop Soviet dirty jokes on a spare cassette, Sergei removing his glasses to wipe the tears from his eyes.

'Why aren't you with the group?' I asked him. 'I thought the Russian circus was supposed to be so marvellous.'

'Not this one!' said Sergei with a gloating chuckle. 'It's a one-tent number from the sticks – three dogs, two goats and an Armenian conjuror.' He will also be avoiding *Swan Lake*, which is promised for tomorrow. '*Swan Lake* on *ice*!' he cackles. 'Silly pricks probably think they're going to the Bolshoi!'

* *

Sunday, 10 August. Sergei's attachment to us is becoming a little embarrassing. Shura is convinced that he is acting on state orders from the K.G.B. both as a spy and an *agent provocateur*. Shura arrived in England from China with a Soviet passport, and their motto is 'Once a Russian, always a Russian'. It is therefore essential that we give him the slip when we go to meet Shura's Moscow friends.

We made nervous contact with the artist Boris Messerer and the beautiful poetess Bella Akmadulina, former wife of the poet Yevtushenko. It was all very cloak and dagger, like 'Meet me under the statue of Karl Marx carrying a Rolling Stones record in a paper bag.' Boris said that he hoped we didn't mind having dinner with his bohemian friends – 'occasion "exprompt", company eclectic'. We said we would be delighted.

The party was given by an architect who lives in a huge high-rise flat on the outskirts of Moscow, not yet finished but already falling down. In a room with plastic wood panelling and chandeliers, a long table is groaning with cold cuts, herrings, gherkins and bottles and bottles of vodka. There are also long-stemmed mushrooms from the woods fried in garlic, chocolate cake and liqueurs. We exchange endless toasts with artists, musicians and architects in workmen's caps and leather jackets, while the gramophone plays 'The Dark Side of the Moon'.

I am still waiting for in-depth conversations about Russian life and intelligent questions about England, but no such luck. All they seem to want to know about is pop music. Do I know Eno and his Roxy Music? Is Andrew Lloyd Webber writing an opera of Gamlet? I look blank. *"Gamlet?"* Shakespeare's Gamlet, of course! I do my best to satisfy them.

After the mushrooms the gentlemen hared down twenty floors, leaped into a freezing reservoir, then came belting back for their cake and coffee.

Later we all went back to Boris's huge studio for more vodka, more music and much embracing and exchanging of gifts.

Boris has a car, but he couldn't take us home. Too many police blocks between here and your hotel, he tells us. Suddenly the whole happy evening turns a trifle sour. On no account will we tell Sergei where we have been.

Saturday, 16 August. We left Moscow for Minsk, and suddenly we were in the Russian countryside of our dreams, the Russia of the fairy stories. Beautiful wooden cottages painted in blue and green with white fretwork round the windows, and sunflowers in the gardens. There are horse-drawn droshkeys, mushroomy woods, geese on the common and women in head scarves kneeling to milk, while their husbands caress the cows' flanks with leafy birch boughs to keep away the flies.

Sergei began to get restless. As we approached the Polish frontier his face got longer and longer, and we could see that something was preying on his mind.

A couple of kilometres before the frontier he took Shura aside, ostensibly to exchange addresses, and tried to force something into his hand. It seems he has a girlfriend in England, and he wanted Shura to take a letter for her. Then, as we reached the frontier, he suddenly said, almost desperately, 'What if I were to make a run for it, to try to reach the other side – would you help me?'

'My dear Sergei,' Shura said patiently, 'why should you want to run from one Communist country to another? And tell me truthfully – do you *really* want me to take this letter for you?'

Sergei, embarrassed and speechless, shook his head. Suddenly a look of vast relief crossed his face – he had done what was expected of him, he had had a go, and now we could be friends again.

'Listen', he said, 'I'll tell you one last Soviet joke. It's not a very funny one actually. There's this little sparrow, see? And along comes a big fat cow and drops a turd right on top of him. Phhttt! "Help," says the sparrow, "I'm drowning, I'm suffocating, but there's nobody to hear." But after a little while he begins to feel warm and cosy and quite at home inside the cow-pat. So he pokes his little head out of the shit and begins to sing.

'Then along comes a hungry old cat, picks him out of the cowpat, cleans him off, and bites his head off.

'Moral one: not all those who drop you in the shit are your enemies.

'Moral two: not all those who pull you out of the shit are your friends.

'Moral three: if you *are* in the shit, keep your head down and don't chirp about it!'

We embraced Sergei warmly and exchanged addresses, although we knew that we would never write, and that if we did he would never answer – Sergei had learnt to keep his head down.

We were still puzzling over the meaning of his last story as we boarded our bus en route for London via Warsaw, East Berlin and Hamburg.

By now I had the travel bug, and after Russia it was America's turn. Our friend June Churchill had been invited to New York to stay with a very grand queen who lived in a brownstone house with wall-to-wall Picassos, and she invited us to come over with her. Not, of course, to stay with this rich queen, but in the grotty old Chelsea Hotel.

However we had one advantage – my niece Catherine Guinness was working for Andy Warhol, so we had access to the famous Factory. After three visits I had still not got a glimpse of the great man, so I was quite excited when Cathy rang up and said she was bringing her boss over for dinner. I rushed over to John Gordon's place and June and I got together a scratch meal of noodles and salad.

In came Andy, a 'bone and a hank of hair'. He had enormous charm and exuded a kind of childlike innocence, but was obviously sharp as a needle. He was taking snaps of everybody with his little camera, and kept calling me 'Catherine's Ant', as if I was some sort of pet insect.

After dinner Andy suggested we all went to Studio Fifty-four, the new, smart place to be seen at. I looked gloomily at my drab, olive-green kaftan, left over from the Sixties – which was fine for an evening at a Health Farm but not quite right for New York's hottest disco. We all piled into a cab and arrived to find a long queue of hopefuls, all looking outrageously trendy, waiting to be vetted by a fearsome-looking doorman. I approached him nervously and saw his lips curl into a derisive sneer as he clocked my greying hair, specs and kaftan. Then Andy got out of the cab and a ripple of excitement ran through the queue. The doorman did a doubletake, then ushered me in as if I was royalty, with Steve Rubell, the minuscule manager, beaming and kissing my hand. It was definitely one of life's better moments.

My other reason for visiting New York was a kind of quest – 'A la Recherche de Tante Perdue', as Shura put it. My Aunt Olivia, better known as Bunch, had always fascinated me. Not only did I look like her, but I had a feeling that our characters were rather similar. She did exactly what she wanted and broke every taboo, and it was my great regret that I had never known her better. Unfortunately she ran away from England and her family when I was quite young and went to live with a black lesbian actress in Harlem.

I had no idea where to start my search until I met an eighty-three-year-old Negro jazz singer called Alberta Hunter in a Village club. She had known Olivia well, and said the man I wanted was Billy Daniels, the former owner of the famous Bon Soir Supper Club in Harlem, who lived quite near the Chelsea Hotel.

I found Billy in a very chic apartment with Thirties decor, flower paintings by Epstein and a friend with shaven head and shades. I was given lashings of gin, and kedgeree for lunch. Olivia, he told me, had deserted a life of grand country houses and show-jumping to join the black actress Edna Thomas, whom she'd seen in *Porgy and Bess*. To get a residency permit she married the tycoon Hoyland Spencer, but immediately deserted him for Edna.

Although she was about the only white woman in Harlem she soon became accepted by the local residents, who called her Lady Olivia, convinced that anyone so eccentric had to be titled. Others called her the Colonel, because she was so bossy. Every now and then she would throw a party, and her more bohemian friends from England would come flocking over – Oliver Messel, Cyril Connolly and the Sitwells, with Cole Porter playing the piano, Gypsy Rose Lee dancing and bootleg gin in the bathtub. Meanwhile my aunt swept around in Grandpa Wyndham's military cape and her tiara, blind as a bat and stubbing out her cigarettes in saucers of caviar. Her main contribution to black culture was bread sauce, Billy said, which can still be sometimes found in Harlem soul restaurants.

Later Edna moved her out to the country to get her away

from drugs and bad company. When her health had recovered she planted an English rose garden and an oak tree which she christened the Duchess of Devonshire.

Olivia died of cancer just before her seventieth birthday, in Billy's arms, and Edna followed her three years later.

I left with my arms full of presents – my aunt's Bible, a pewter mug, a framed photograph of the young Olivia with an Eton crop dressed as a sailor, and my grandfather's war medals.

I came home to find that Clare, my eldest daughter, who had been working in Newcastle as a model for several years, had become engaged to a Portuguese called Joachim. They had rosy visions of finding a small farm somewhere, of self-sufficiency and the good life. They finally realised their dreams in an old Tuscan farmhouse where they looked after the vines and olives for the local landlord. They also imported macrobiotic food-stuffs which they optimistically hoped to flog to the locals.

There were dogs, cats, pigs, chickens, ducks and pigeons, a huge vegetable plot and barns full of brown rice and fermenting soya sauce.

It was with some trepidation that I planned my first visit. I was extremely keen to make a good impression on Joachim, but I had a vague suspicion that my reputation as a hard-drinking bohemian lady had probably preceded me.

Oh well, I thought on the first evening, one small whisky a day won't do me any harm! I poured one out from my secret stash, and filled it to the brim from a bottle marked Vichy water which was sitting in the fridge. Little did I know that it was a present of home-brewed grappa from the peasant next door. Quite strong for a single, I thought, as I knocked it back – which was not surprising as the damn stuff must have been about 140 proof. Half an hour later I fell flat on my face during some home movies of a holiday in Mauritius, and had to be carried to bed by Clare and my future son-in-law, whose worse suspicions had now been confirmed.

It wasn't until I reached for the water bottle the following morning that all was discovered and my reputation saved.

From there I went on to join Cammy in Cadaques, a little

village in Spain where we had rented a villa. It was very near to Port Lligat, so we were all hoping to catch a glimpse of Salvador Dali. Weeks went by without a sign of the great man, and we were getting very bored. Cadaques had no beach, just rocks covered in sea-urchins, and as there was also a howling gale we couldn't sunbathe. Cammy became so bored she even had an affair with a married man. She hoped to keep it a secret but unfortunately gave him her cold, which soon gave the game away as they sniffled their way round the bars and night clubs. In despair she even took to going out dancing with me, but that too was not a great success as everybody thought we were lesbians. Then one day our luck changed. We met a beautiful young man on the beach, who invited us to have drinks with Dali.

We set off for Port Lligat dressed in what we considered suitable outfits – me in a flowing white kaftan, Cammy in sun top and long Victorian lace-trimmed knickers. Dali met us on the terrace and led us through labyrinthine corridors to a small sitting room. 'Cherie?' he asked tentatively. A brown withered arm shot up from behind a small settee and the hand wiggled its long blood-red nails at him. As we rounded the settee we saw a skinny woman in black toreador pants, with a big Minnie Mouse bow set on top of her head like ears. She put out her hand in greeting, then pulled it away before we could touch it, never ceasing to glare at us with her dark penetrating eyes. From then on she ignored us completely, speaking only to two young male models called the Heavenly Twins who sat like acolytes at her feet. This must be Gala, I thought, and a rather scary lady she seemed too.

Luckily Dali was just the opposite, enormously friendly and talking non-stop. Unlike most people who do this he didn't only talk about himself, but seemed interested in other people and asked us a lot of questions, mostly unanswerable or unintelligible.

A maid in a proper uniform brought pink champagne, and we gave Dali our present, a pair of joke spectacles with bloodshot eyeballs that shot out on springs. He was most appreciative. Later he showed Cammy his studio, and asked her if she would sit for him the following day.

She found Dali in a long Chinese coat and floppy hat

languishing on his satin 'lips' sofa in the garden. Later they went into the studio, Dali very excited about a new painting of his which was designed to be seen through 3D glasses – when you put them on all sorts of weird creatures leapt out of the undergrowth.

She stood naked by the window, leaning on the sill, with a constant audience of tourists in the street below exclaiming 'Gee, look at that girl – does he keep her there all the time?'

It was terribly hot, and after an hour the pose became excruciatingly painful and her legs started trembling from lack of circulation, but she didn't dare say anything. In any case normal communication was difficult, as his answers to questions were not only surreal and irrelevant, but couched in a mixture of Spanish, French and English.

An occasional stolen glance at the drawing showed her with a tiny nipped-in waist and huge bottom. The floor was literally covered in sketches – she could see her footprints on some of them – and she kept thinking that if only she was wearing knickers she could have stuffed some inside them. Any hope of getting one from Dali was doomed, as Gala kept a beady eye on his generosity.

What Cammy finally got was a signed poster and a bunch of artificial apricots, which he said reminded him of her. She took this for a compliment until he explained that they reminded him of her blonde fuzzy legs! She also got a single Moroccan slipper. 'Two slippers you might lose,' he told her in his usual cryptic fashion, 'one slipper you will never lose!' He was quite right, of course – it's still in her underwear drawer.

Chapter Ten

$\mathcal{N}$ I arrived back at Wellington Square one summer's day in 1978 to find a strange young man lurking in Camilla's basement flat – my cousin Charlie Tennant, a nervous, skinny boy with huge eyes. He lived on chocolates and banana milk.

His father, Colin Tennant, had given him some money to start a magazine called *The Chelsea Scoop,* which he hoped would distract him from more harmful pursuits. Charlie, and the rather unfortunately named Nigel Coke, were running it from my basement. They had got a very funny interview with Andy Warhol for the first edition, but were desperately in need of more copy, so they had asked me to come up with something juicy.

Luckily an American friend called Mankow was in London. He was the author of an erotic guidebook called *Lusty Europe,* and skimming through it I came across the address of Jan Bik, who ran Amsterdam's biggest erotic centre. His latest venture was called Callboy International, and catered for ladies who were 'past the grand climacteric', as he so charmingly put it.

I'd always been interested in the idea of male tarts for women and thought it grossly unfair that men should have access to easy uncomplicated sex, whilst we had only two alternatives – monogamous fidelity or ghastly affairs that nearly always ended in heartbreak. I also liked the idea of being dominant and telling some gorgeous boy to do exactly what I wanted. There was, of course, an obvious snag – the small mechanical difficulty of the man having to get an erection. How did they cope with old, and possibly ugly, women? I was determined to find out, and rang up Jan Bik in Amsterdam, telling him I was a journalist who wanted to come out and do a story for a magazine. He was very affable and offered to put me up in his brothel, but I decided to opt for a hotel by the canal.

Next I roped in my friend Dolly Frankel, as I was far too scared to go alone. Dolly, who kept open house in Wembley Park, and was always game for anything, wanted to know if we would actually have to *do* it! No, I said firmly, you'll just talk to the boys and interview their clients – a nice, straightforward piece of investigative journalism. I thought Dolly sounded a mite disappointed.

Friday 8 June. We boarded the night train for Amsterdam in the pouring rain, heavily hung about with cameras and tape recorders. Dolly was trying hard to look like a real journalist in her 80p Bogart mac from Oxfam with matching Noddy rainhat. Even her umbrella had newsprint on it, in memory no doubt of those halcyon days in the WAAF when she was a sub-editor on the *Orkney Blast*.

On the train we compiled a list of questions for the boys worthy of Masters and Johnson, including the 10,000-guilder one – 'In view of the fact that a lot of the ladies may be old and unattractive, how do you get it up?' (or 'opp', as the Dutch say).

Saturday, 9 June. The sun greets us as we check into our small canal-side hotel, a bit nervous lest it prove a bourgeois Dutch family-type operation, hostile to our research. We needn't have worried. As we go upstairs to our room, we hear with relief the unmistakable accents of the Middle West: 'Hey, Alice! Have you cleaned the fuckin' bath?' and out pops the manager, a young bearded American in a T-shirt.

We phone our underworld contacts from the foyer, but the staff's ears are pricked. In no time at all, there's a knock on the door and it's the manager.

'Couldn't help hearing what you ladies are up to. I was wondering – maybe you could help me get a call-boy job myself? I sure could use the extra bread!'

It is obvious that he means this seriously. We ask him the Big Question.

'Get it "opp"? Oh easy – just get stoned out of my mind!'

Somewhat stunned at the speed at which things are proceeding, we promise to put in a good word for him and set out for Bik's brothel to conduct our first interview.

'Do you realise,' I say to Dolly as we knock on the Harrlemerdyk door, 'that the last time I was in Amsterdam was in 1962, photographing Miss Edam Cheese for *Housewife* magazine?'

Bik, a small, bouncy, bearded guy who looks like a philosophy professor (which he previously was) ushers us into his den. Through deepest gloom, we can make out a huge couch in mock ocelot, a small desk with a telephone and a candy jar full of Durex, with a plastic mermaid on the lid. There is also a huge map of Holland with hundreds of little flags, each one pin-pointing the whereabouts of part-time 'housewifewhores' – women, usually married, who work from home with their husbands' full consent. Upstairs, there's a spotless bar, a projector for blue films, a few bored-looking 'girls' playing liar dice, and five bedrooms where it all happens.

J: 'Tell us Herr Bik – '

BIK: 'Call me Jan – '

J: 'Tell us about this call boy service for women.'

BIK: 'Well, the boys are no problem – I have offers every week. But many of the women play hard to get. They are convinced they can only sleep with a man if they like him – almost *never* will a lady confess she only wants sex just for an hour.

J: 'But there must be hundreds of frustrated ladies who would happily pay!'

BIK: 'Oh no, if a lady *really* needs sex, she can get it at any time with a wink of the eye in town – for free!'

J: 'What about the really shy ones?'

BIK: 'They'd be too shy to come to me anyway. No, I tell you, it is rather a difficult business – the only boys who make their daily bread from it are the real professional hunters, the playboys who specialise in making a lady fall in love. Then she'll give the boy an apartment, a Porsche – but she doesn't like to give just money. We have tried brothels with boys – never a success! Just an orgasm is not enough for a lady – and in any case how many women are enjoying their orgasm at that age, fifty to sixty?' (Dolly and I exchanged amazed looks.)

J: 'As members of that age group we can assure you ...!'

BIK: (Politely) 'You are so old?'

J: 'Fifty-five and -six respectively.'

'Bravo! You look really very well on it,' cries Bik, and rings the bell for drinks. Enter gorgeous brunette in pink harem pants with ice-cold Dutch gin and beer chasers. While we drink, Bik shows us some letters from prospective boys.

BIK: 'Here's a twenty-one-year-old Indonesian. "I want to do everything to spoil ladies and take good care of them so that they may have beautiful sex remembering of me." '

J: 'How sweet! And how sad that the women don't want him!'

A knock on the door and in come two butch guys in sheepskin jackets. 'Call boys?' we ask hopefully.

BIK: 'No, they've come to lay the carpet. Pauli, Pieter, meet Dolly and Joan, fifty-six and fifty-eight, American journalists!'

D: '*Fifty-five, fifty-six, and English,* if you don't mind,' but Jan takes no notice. This is our label and we're stuck with it.

Enter burly dungareed electrician and salesman with wallpaper samples – it's getting like a Marx Brothers film.

BIK: 'Wolfgang, Hans, meet Dolly and Joan,' and soon we are helping to choose tasteful florals for the upstairs bedrooms, while knocking back gin and chasers. It's all great fun but our call boy article is getting nowhere, and we are just about to leave when the door bursts open and in comes a lean, black-haired, tight-trousered, six-foot Adonis, wearing heavy silver bracelets and a gold mounted shark's tooth round his neck.

'Oh boy! Have you ladies fallen with your noses in the butter!' crows Jan. 'This is Erik, the best Dutch playboy in town, a real hunter! Erik, meet Dolly – '

Erik looks languidly bored, then his practised eyes zoom in like radar beams on Dolly's Cartier watch. He brightens visibly. His eyes do a quick carat-calculation on her gold chains and appear to find them satisfactory – me, in crumpled jeans and Berber jewellery, he quite rightly ignores as poor bohemian trash. He pulls out a packet of American cigarettes, and Dolly gives him a light.

ERIK: 'Dupont!'

D: 'How do you know it's not an imitation?' Erik gives her a look of withering professional scorn.

ERIK: 'Oh, come! One can always tell a Dupont – it has that completely distinctive click. One has to know to whom one is talking, otherwise one can waste so much time.'

J: 'Tell us about yourself, Erik. Have you always lived off women?'

ERIK: 'Ever since I was sixteen. I have *never* worked! Why should I?' He pulls out a wad of 1,000–guilder notes from a crocodile case. 'Mind you, it's hard work. Last night I had to keep it up for nearly three hours – but boy, was it worth it! Her husband,' he adds in a tone of deepest respect, 'runs a mink farm.'

D: 'What do you like best in women?'

ERIK: 'Apart from money? Oh, high social class – that turns me on. Personality more than looks. They must not be boring! Beautiful middle-aged women are best. Young girls, *forget* it! Such tantrums, jealousies, drug troubles, fatiguing demands! I like a nice older woman who's quiet and relaxed and has been through all the shit.'

J: 'But suppose you decide to make it with someone *really* old? How do you get it up?'

ERIK: 'I drink, I fantasise, I put cocaine under my fingernails, it goes everywhere! But mostly I think of the money!'

D: 'How much money?'

ERIK: 'It depends on how ugly she is. If she is really ugly a *great deal* of money!'

J: 'And how do you approach them?'

ERIK: 'Oh, it must happen very casually – we get friendly, I take her out for a few drinks, perhaps a meal – all this is an investment, you understand – then later, I tell her frankly, "Look, I'm for sale. I'm expensive! But I give very good value, and I cook good too!" So then they go or stay. The worst is when a woman *pretends* to be rich – you waste all this time and money on her and she has nothing! *Nothing!* Ah well! The hazards of the trade!'

J: 'And what is your ultimate goal?'

ERIK: 'A rich marriage of course. A millionairess. Then I will

have the big Rolls Royce and the house in Paddington.'
(Paddington!?)

Erik exits, offering to show us the town, but we decline, fearing it might prove a little expensive.

'Come back Friday and I'll show you a *working* night,' promises Jan as we stagger out of the brothel, amazed to find it still daylight.

Sunday, 10 June. Nice breakfast of smoked cheese and currant bread, discussing which to visit first, the mixed sauna or Sunny Call-Boys. (American family at next table torn between Anne Frank's house and the Cheese Market listen fascinated.) Sunny Boys wins – we don't feel our figures are quite up to the sauna – and Doll rings to make an appointment.

It's way out in the suburbs. We lose our way, take the wrong bus, finally toil up five flights of stairs to No. 616. Two ravishing young men in white answer the bell and look at us in utter consternation. It appears they were expecting two *male* punters – Dolly's voice on the phone being a trifle butch – so they'd been showering and slapping on the Brut and ironing their jeans only to open the door on their worst dream come true – two ladies who look like their mothers, with tape-recorders!

It takes a lot of vivacious chat about their lovely plants and their divine cats to calm them down and make them accept us enough to usher us into the bedroom of Mr Sunny Boy himself, a handsome forty-ish guy with dyed blond hair, who is in bed with ulcer trouble. He's called Henny, and he runs a stable of boys who cater for men and women alike.

J: 'How do your women clients choose a boy? Do you show them photographs?'

SB: 'No, the boy goes to the home, and I tell them, if he is not right, you can send him back and not pay – you only pay if it clicks!'

D: 'How much?'

SB: 'One seventy-five guilders for one contact, and they take as much time as they like. If the customer is very nice, and gives them wine and coffee and the television is good or they have nice records, the boy stays a long time.'

D: 'And suppose the boy doesn't like the customer?'

SB: 'I tell the boy, if you can't do it, come back! Sometimes he comes into my sleeping room and cries! I have a boy, seventeen, he comes back crying, "I can do nothing to this lady, she has a leg in wood which she takes off!"'

D: 'How awful!'

SB: 'Yes, I have to take such a boy for one week out and send him for a rest by the seaside, perhaps a nice easy escort job with no sex.'

J: 'Do *any* attractive women apply?'

SB: 'Almost never – but it doesn't matter if she is old or ugly provided she is fresh and clean! The boys only think of the money, they close their eyes and their ears, into the bed one hour and is going! Full time boys make good money, 1,000 guilders a week – but I have one rule, discretion. Any boy who talks is *out*. All my addresses are in code, so there is no fear of blackmail.'

Gin and beer arrive and we all get pleasantly sloshed. Dolly announces that it is her birthday today.

SB: 'Really? It's our Queen's birthday too!'

We all cheer, vibrators buzz, condoms are tossed in the air – Dolly gets one as a birthday present – and the assembled boys sing 'Happy Birthday to You'.

'Tell me, what do *women* look for in a boy?' I continue, getting back to business.

SB: 'Big guys with muscles who come many times, guys with big "*luls*".'

D: 'Big what?'

SB: 'Lyon–Utrecht–Lyon! Lul!'

'The big prick,' Peter puts in helpfully.

J: 'Not pretty boys like you?'

P: 'No, I am for the gentlemen. But if I *had* to have a lady, I would want to have a nice boy in the room behind a screen to excite me first.'

D: 'Well, I suppose we ought to be going – unless you've got any more questions, Joan?'

J: 'No, I rather think that after all that stuff about how they cry on Henny's shoulder, and wooden legs and so on, we might as well skip the last ten questions about whether they love and revere older ladies and form deep meaningful relationships with them.'

We part the best of friends. Henny gives us an ad to place for him in magazines in England. It reads 'Gentlemen watch!

Relax in your home and through hole of Holland boys will come and please you discreet.'

D: 'Through *hole?* Oh, the *whole* of Holland! I think I should re-word that if I were you.'

Monday, 11 June. Hank, the manager, pops in after breakfast to hear tapes and to see whether we've managed to get him a job yet. We tell him it's difficult, the profession seems a bit over-crowded. Our last tape is a disaster, starting well but disintegrating after the arrival of the gin into hysterical laughter, gurgles and splashes, Dutch oaths and then total silence as I press the wrong button on the microphone.

D: 'So what shall we do today?'

J: 'How about testing out Bik's theory that any woman can pick up a boy for free if she really tries?'

D: 'OK, so how do we go about it?'

J: 'Well, I've heard there's a place called the Milky Way bursting at the seams with lovely boys. Also, the dope is legal there.'

Half an hour later, we're in a huge converted warehouse. Dolly has a look of nervous expectancy on her face as a red-haired transvestite with five o'clock shadow tattoos her arm for re-entry. She is still wearing the Noddy hat. 'Take that bloody thing off or I won't go in with you,' I hiss. 'And, for Christ's sake, try to look a bit more cool. This is the Melkweg Multi-Media Complex, not the Brent Cross shopping centre!'

Inside, we pass through a huge room full of stalls selling everything from organically-grown apricots to hash sticks, and find the coffee bar. Through a dense cloud of marijuana, we dimly perceive several hundred young people happily rolling joints – with the government's blessing. It all looks a trifle grubby after the sparkling cleanliness of the brothels we've visited. Dolly's face brightens at the sight of a bar laden with homemade food. I settle her down opposite two black boys, and go off in search of organic banana crumble and goat's milk yoghurt. By the time I come back she is beginning to slide gently beneath the table, a glazed look in her eyes and a large joint sticking out of her mouth.

'Where can I buy some of this lovely stuff?' she asks the beaming boys as she hands the joint to me.

'Come on, Dolly,' I say firmly, 'no one's going to proposition us here, they're all too stoned. What we need is a little culture.' So we went to the Van Gogh Museum, collapsed in a comfortable seat in front of *The Sunflowers*, and fell asleep till closing time.

Tuesday, 12 June. Wake at midday longing for cold beer. Bik had recommended a floating bordello, the Mother Julia, just a few hundred yards down the canal – it had a bar, so there we went. The door of the houseboat was opened by a character straight out of Irma La Douce – leather jacket, two-tone suedette cap, high-heeled boots, and piercingly beautiful eyes. Frank runs a very tight little ship, with three resident boys, wall-to-wall red flock wallpaper, and a few bijou bedrooms for the customers. Yet again, everything is dazzlingly clean and suburban, with toile de Jouey duvet covers and little fake fur hats on the loo seats. Frank also turns out to be surprisingly prudish.

F: 'You know, it is all the fault of those dreadful porn magazines – without them there would be no need for my profession! Giving people all sorts of kinky ideas about funny positions and chains and black suspenders and so on, when they could be having a good solid Dutch marriage.'

D: 'Do you have any sidelines?'

F: 'Well, I once ran an answering service for heavy breathers. That was a really nice operation, no sweat, no overheads. Unfortunately, it fell through because the breathers didn't like having to book their calls. They said it spoilt the spontaneity of the thing.'

In the evening we went back to Bik's brothel. 'We won't stay long,' I said to Dolly. 'I really feel like an early night.' Five hours and numerous gins later we're both still there. Dolly is downstairs with Jan monitoring the customers, I'm upstairs in the bar with the 'ladies', pop-eyed in front of a blue film. This is a Climax Production entitled, *tout simplement*, Mr Big Cock, starring a skinny little guy staggering under the weight of his aforementioned asset. Sitting around the cosy bar in comfortable armchairs are a number of bored-looking punters who have obviously seen the film before, and four friendly tarts, chosen to suit all tastes – one large-bosomed matronly type, strapless in sequins, a scrubbed-looking girl-next-door in jeans, a cool slinky black girl, and one far-out bitch queen with dark glasses, punk rock haircut and diamanté stilettoes.

They insist on treating me to another reel; this time schoolgirls, spanking, dildos and dykes. I begin to feel a bit sick – is it the gin, or is it the sight of all those under-age bottoms bobbing remorselessly up and down to the rhythm of 'It ain't what you do it's the way that you do it?'

Walking carefully, I negotiate the narrow stairs to Jan's office. Dolly is standing pinned to the wall by the hypnotic power of Jan, who, cool and professional, prowls around her, sizing her up as a potential housewife whore. He is running his hands expertly over every curve, patting and pinching her like some prize cow, and finally raises her arm like a railway signal to steal a quick sniff, Dolly being too paralysed by surprise to resist.

'Not bad! Not bad at all for fifty-eight,' he chortles, 'the legs good, the tits good, the eyes a little old perhaps – *hot verdomme!* she really turns me on, your friend! You have seen her without the clothes, yes? How is she, OK? How is the skin?'

'Fine, just fine, great!' I cry, catching Dolly's glare.

BIK: 'Of course, she would have to smarten herself up a little if she worked for me.'

The phone rings. 'Bik Erotic Centre? No, no, I do not think this is for me. Perhaps you try Monique Van Cleef's House of Torture, or the Chapel of Satan.'

The traffic is quite brisk now, with clients hot-footing it up the stairs and Bik in his little white woolly socks leaping up like a mountain goat onto his desk to check up on their files. Suddenly he hears the sound of descending steps, and bounds into the hall, bowing and rubbing his hands like a maitre d'.

BIK: 'And how was it, Minheer? You like Maxie? She was satisfactory? Perhaps next time you try Zazie?'

Maxie comes down the stairs behind him – she is clutching herself in mock anguish with one hand, and her loot with the other.

'Is it worth it?' she asks the world in general as she stuffs the guilders into her bag and slips on her coat to go home to hubby.

BIK: 'Ah, these part-time housewives are not really professional! Now Zazie is such a pro that she won't even allow the customer to *enter* her!'

He splashes half a pint of Eau Savage under each armpit and does a few press-ups. 'I am an ex-gymnast – I like to keep in shape,' he explains.

J: 'But tell me, are most of the housewife whores like Maxie just doing it to buy a colour TV but not really enjoying it?'

BIK: 'Oh, not at all. I have one lady about your age – Anna – she enjoys up to twenty orgasms a night. How many orgasms do *you* have, by the way?'

After this polite enquiry he does a backward somersault, raising himself like a tiny banking aeroplane on one hand, his eyes glinting beadily upwards through his round specs.

Dolly and I quickly change the subject, fearing we are not in Anna's league.

J: 'So what's the going rate here?'

BIK: 'One hundred guilders an hour – without extras.'

D: 'What sort of extras?'

BIK: 'Sadism, masochism, anal intercourse and swallowing sperm – you cannot expect this from the general women in Europe, so it is 150 extra. I warn the girls first, because Greeks always think anal intercourse is normal, Americans that French things are normal – '

J: 'And the English?'

BIK: 'Oh, they like best spanking! To *be* spanked I mean, by the stern governess. They want just down with the trousers, bom, bom, bom! ten or twenty times on the backside and finish.'

J: 'And they have an orgasm that way?'

BIK: 'Of course, it is very quick with most of them, just trousers down, bom, bom, bom and off!'

D: 'Why do you do this kind of work, Jan?'

BIK: 'First, because I like it, second, for my bread. And third, I am doing much more good things than I could in any other profession. I think many doctors, priests and psychiatrists can do more harm to people than I can.'

We arrive back at the hotel at 3 am, total wrecks, cold and tired – all we want is a nice cup of tea and, if possible, a hot-water bottle. There's a light in the manager's room. Dolly knocks on his door and he says 'Sure, tea up in a trice!'

Sighing with pleasure, we leap into bed, Dolly in a high-necked winceyette number, a passion-killer second only to the Noddy hat. Ten minutes later, up comes Hank, not only with tea tray but also with a lithe, swarthy, moustachioed friend, a sub-Omar Sharif in total black leather. He sits on my bed and rakes us both with his beady eyes. We sip our tea in embarrassed silence. Hank leaps into the breach, having obviously received some secret go-ahead signal.

H: 'Carlos here would – er – really dig to have a scene with you two ladies.'

D: '*Both* of us? A threesome?'

H: 'Well, not exactly, more like a foursome. You see, I've been watching you ladies and not only do I think you're a couple of fantastic birds, but if I'm going into the call boy business it's a good idea for me to have a bit of practice with older women.'

D: (A bit thrown by this) 'How much would it – er – cost?'

H: 'Nothing – on the house, be my guests!'

Us: (In unison) 'Freebies!'

H: 'So it's on? Great!'

Dolly and I look at one another ...

I wish I could tell you that there followed a wild orgy worthy of Climax Productions, but, alas, I cannot tell a lie. Five minutes later, after the boys had bid us a reluctant goodnight, we were alone once more, clutching our hot-water bottles. Minutes passed. Dolly broke the silence.

D: 'Do you realise that we have just turned down *300 guilders'* worth? It must be the first bargain I've ever turned down in my life?'

J: 'Why do you think they reckoned we were amenable?'

D: 'I'll tell you exactly why. Remember that night he came up here and I was saying *I* didn't think women wanted casual sex, *you* came out with that unforgettable line – "All over Britain, frustrated women in their thousands are *writhing on their beds.*" '

J: (Pensively) 'Ah yes, it could have been that. He reckoned us for a couple of writhers.'

D: 'As a matter of interest, who do you think would have had whom?'

J: 'Oh, Hank was after you, I'd have been lumbered with Omar Sharif.'

I turn the light off.

J: 'Sad, isn't it, three days and nights spent in Europe's sexiest city and here we are with our hot-water bottles and a nice cup of tea.'

D: 'I wouldn't worry, darling – not a soul is going to believe us.'

Chapter Eleven

Compared to the hectic Sixties, my life during the Seventies seemed a reasonably easy game to play. The dice rolled in my favour and ladders far outnumbered the snakes.

Amazingly enough we were still dancing.

Our friend Michael Fish had opened a wonderful new club called the Embassy. It was not overtly gay, in spite of waiters in satin shorts on roller skates, and older ladies like June Churchill and I were definitely welcome. We may have looked like a couple of silly old fruit-flies as 'Freak Out' blared from the speakers and we were whirled through the laser beams by our gay popper-snorting escorts, but we didn't care – we were having a ball. (Poppers – or amyl-nitrate, which you could get from the chemists by faking a bad heart – were now all the rage with trendies, who wouldn't be seen dead smoking a joint.)

By the law of averages it was now time for another snake, and one was already slithering through the undergrowth.

It all started after a fantastic meal at an Italian restaurant called Leonardo's. Cammy and I had just discovered starch blockers, a miracle pill which was supposed to let you eat all the fattening things you liked without putting on weight, and we had gone to town with starch for every course.

I attributed my nasty stomach pains to spinach lasagne followed by spaghetti vongole and suppa inglese, but after they had continued for over a week I got a bit worried.

When antibiotics had failed to do any good, my GP referred me to a specialist, and then began the big medical charade as each Harley Street pundit in turn plugged his own speciality.

'Almost certainly a case of irritable bowel syndrome,' said Dr A. 'Verticulitis,' said Dr B. 'Stress,' said the psychiatrist. 'Pelvic Inflammatory Disease,' said Dr D. Dr E. was not a hundred per cent sure but he thought it might be referred pain from the back, and sent me to his good friend Dr F., who was at least honest. 'Nothing wrong at all with your back,' he snapped. 'That will be fifty five guineas, please.' Dr G., the only completely honest one of the lot, diagnosed an advanced case of GOK – God only knows.

Six months later, and still in dreadful pain, I decided to test out their theories with an exploratory operation. As we were on BUPA, I was booked into a luxurious room in an extremely expensive hospital, with an Arab sheikh on one side and David Niven on the other.

On the first day a little Irish nurse handed me an enormously long menu which would have done credit to the Ritz.

'Well,' I said gleefully, 'I think I'll start with the Beluga caviar, go on to the Boeuf Wellington and finish with a few fresh strawberries.'

'Oh no you won't!' said the staff nurse, bustling in purposefully and slapping a notice on my bed saying 'Nothing by Mouth.'

'Stick the caviar in the fridge,' I managed to hiss in the ear of my little nurse as I was given my barium enema.

The next thing I knew I was lying on a white couch with an extremely handsome doctor bending over me. On a screen overhead there was a riveting picture of the barium enema progressing slowly through my innards. I've always had a thing about handsome doctors, and gazed up soulfully into his eyes. He responded with a deep, meaningful look.

'Mrs Shivarg,' he breathed, 'you have the bowels of a teenager!'

So much for doctors A. and B. Somewhat relieved I hurried back to my room, to find my husband waiting for me and together we raided the fridge for Caviar.

Two days later, after numerous X-rays and a cat scan, I finally had an exploratory operation, and the surgeon announced triumphantly that he had found a rather large gallstone of a most peculiar shape, which was undoubtedly the cause of the trouble. I was to go immediately to his colleague, Dr H., who had arranged to whip it out. I was over the moon – at last a genuine diagnosis! But it was not to be.

'I've look at the X-rays,' said Dr H., looking puzzled and slightly embarrassed, 'and quite frankly I can't see any signs at all of a gallstone. Of course, I *could* cut you open just in case –'

'No, no!' I cried, making hastily for the door, and that was the end of my long entanglement with conventional medicine.

I now decided to try out the alternatives, and went to see Robin Dee, a well-known clairvoyant.

'You have a pain which comes and goes,' he pronounced, 'but no doctor can cure it – it is called a Miasma, the ghost of a pain suffered in some former life by one of your ancestors. It is as if a bell has been struck and the sound is still reverberating – try a psychic healer.' I had never heard of a Miasma before, but nevertheless I decided to consult a certain Mr Tonaka, a gigantic Japanese in a wig who lived in north London. In spite of his nationality the atmosphere in his consulting-room was extremely Indian, with joss sticks burning in front of a photograph of his guru, and lots of 'Hari, Hari' on the tape recorder.

'You have an extremely powerful and malevolent ancestor lodged in your thorax,' he murmured, as he swung his pendulum over me, 'but I will attempt to clear him out.'

After a few more sessions and much laying on of hands, he asked if I drank coffee.

'Yes, lots!' I replied.

'Good!' said Tonaka. 'Every morning you must boil up your coffee for three minutes, strain it through some fine muslin, let it cool and then give it to yourself in the form of an enema.'

The idea of brewing up my precious breakfast coffee and then sticking it up my bottom was more than I could take, so I went instead to an osteopath who attached me to something resembling an electric octopus with suction pads, and told me to try alternate applications of hot water compresses and packs of frozen peas. I ended up eating an awful lot of Bird's Eye petit pois, but felt no better.

It was then that my friend Jilly told me about a very high-powered physician from Tibet who lived in darkest Neasden. By now I was willing to try anything.

At the Tibetan's house I was greeted by a barefoot girl and a strong smell of vegetable curry. Upstairs the sage was sitting in a long embroidered gown, with his interpreter cross-legged on the floor at his feet. I don't know whether it was this rather uncomfortable posture or maybe the beans in the vegetable curry, but our consultation was punctuated by the interpreter's gentle and continued farts, which didn't seem to embarrass him at all.

The physician measured my fingers with little bits of paper and after a few questions he told me I was suffering from what the Tibetans call 'a disease of the cold' – the current running around the lower part of my body had frozen up and was causing a blockage. I was given a list of 'cold foods' to avoid, and told to wrap my loins in fur during the winter.

'Rabbit fur will do nicely,' said the physician, 'but yeti fur is better!'

I realised from the way that the interpreter was falling about (with disastrously flatulent results) that this was meant to be a Tibetan joke, so I laughed dutifully and went home with a cloth bag full of what looked like large brown horse pills.

The pills did me no good at all, and in despair, I booked myself in for a healing week at the Rajneesh ashram in Suffolk. This was run by the so-called Orange People, followers of the Baghwan – he of the fifteen Rolls Royces. According to the popular press they were into mad orgies of free love, so I didn't know quite what to expect.

I packed a bag of suitable clothes, all in muted shades of orange, pink and maroon. My taxi was stopped at a guarded gate in a barbed wire fence, and we were passed through to a reception hut run by a nice lady in a pink jump suit. (Pink and red, as well as orange, were by then considered acceptable Rajneesh colours.) Outside in the garden I could see couples standing like statues locked in each other's arms – a static version of the famous Rajneesh 'hug'. Everybody hugged each other all the time because they were not allowed to kiss. Although Aids was practically ignored in the West at that time, the Bhagwan was convinced that it would be the next great plague of the earth, so he forbad his followers to have oral sex or even to kiss – hence the prevalence of hugging!

The first thing I saw after being shown to my icy-cold, white chalet was a pair of rubber gloves hanging by the sink – 'to be used for fore-play'. It seemed that love in the commune was not a load of fun, in spite of newspaper stories to the contrary. No kissing, no oral or anal sex, and as they all slept in dormitories, not an awful lot of anything.

With some trepidation I braved the main building, a seething mass of pink, red and orange huggers, and found, thank God, a bar – not a health-juice bar but a proper bar, selling whisky, with people talking about football. I downed a large one and lit up a fag.

'Don't puff that poison in my face,' said the barman petulantly. 'This bar is my place of worship, and you're polluting it for me.' Apparently all their work is called 'worship' – which is just as well as they seem to do plenty of it.

In the middle of the bar area, a girl was sitting crying her eyes out, flanked by two female huggers. I ordered another whisky and sat down near her.

'You mustn't worry about Hari Poojam,' a hugger told her. 'I'm sure he'll come back to you in the end.'

'He won't, he won't!' wailed the girl. 'He came to me this morning and told me he didn't have any more energy for me!'

After a bit she quietened down and said she had to go, because she was worshipping in the kitchen, and I went off to have my first meal.

I had been put onto raw food, which consisted of a beautifully composed salad with the word 'love' spelt out on top of it in pistachio nuts. Everybody else seemed to be eating hamburgers and baked beans, which struck me as odd until someone told me that they had a junk food night once a week.

After dinner we settled down in the living room in acute discomfort to listen to videos of the Bhagwan. He seemed a very humorous fellow, who talked a lot of sense, made rather bad jokes and interlined his speech with strange hissing noises – maybe there was something wrong with his teeth. Luckily I was near the door and was able to crab-crawl my way out after the first video.

The morning began early with howls and screams from the

hut next door, where the disciples, known as Sannyasin, were having their first meditation of the day – the Dynamic. The girls were in long robes, the men stripped to the waist and masked. For fifteen minutes they hyperventilated, shouting 'Hoo hoo!', falling about, screaming and generally releasing their inner conflicts. Whenever the music stopped they had to stand stock still for a further fifteen minutes in the position they were caught in, rather like 'Grandmother's Footsteps'. The trick was not to get caught with one leg in the air.

After breakfast, we outsiders were allowed in to dance. It was only nine o'clock in the morning but already we were hurling ourselves around to oriental music – it felt really far out, as they said there. (Yes, they still talked like hippies.)

After dancing we got our treatment. The most enjoyable one involved being given a pillow and told to thump it, pretending it was your husband, or anybody else who had given you aggro. We were encouraged to scream and utter obscenities, but I was too embarrassed to give more than the occasional shout of satisfaction as I bashed Shura's face into a pulp.

Others were not so reticent and their howls occasionally pierced the walls. This was rather unfortunate as a group of local nurses and Japanese businessmen were being given a guided tour of the commune, and had just settled down for a promotional talk in the foyer.

'Whatever the press may say, we are a peaceful, hard-working community,' said the lady in the pink jumpsuit. 'All those stupid stories about midnight orgies are quite, *quite* untrue!'

'Fuck you!' came loud and clear through the wall from the next door room, followed by frenzied grunts and thumps. After the second expletive the stunned Japs and nurses were hastily shepherded off to see the laundry. This was a large shed labelled 'Beloved's Whizz-Wash', with lots of pink, red and orange clothing – none of it colour-fast – going in one end and coming out the other an indeterminate shade of sludgy tan.

After something called Bodywork – an agonizing torture dealt out by the bony fingers of a sadistic Swede – I was sent to a disciple called Prem for some meditation. He asked me what I felt I was most in need of, so I said I would like the spiritual equivalent of two Valium and a large whisky. Prem was not sure that he could manage that, but he gave me instead some deep breathing exercises and a mantra to recite a hundred times.

After dinner a new Sannyasin was initiated into the movement. We listened to a taped message from the Bhagwan, a necklace with 'His' picture on it was hung round the initiate's neck, and an inordinate amount of hugging took place. Then the band broke into the most wonderfully exciting music – like Russian gypsy, only wilder. We all danced like maniacs until the early hours, and I found myself involved in an extremely exciting hugging session with a ginger-bearded Sannyasin who obviously didn't believe kissing would give him Aids.

I found the Rajneeshis an exceptionally friendly and quite normal lot, apart from their belief that Bhagwan is God. Unfortunately, a few weeks after I left, the centre in Oregon went down in a welter of attempted murder, poisoned needles, robbery and arson, and the Bhagwan was committed to prison for U.S. immigration offences. So this was the only time I was able to visit the ashram.

Alas, the good effects of this healing week were short-lived, and soon the miasma was back again. I began to think seriously about the words of my Japanese healer – maybe some unfortunate ancestor was haunting me, and needed to be exorcised.

After much research, we finally tracked down a certain Dr Macnab, who specialises in getting rid of troublesome earthbound ancestors.

Macnab's house was in the middle of the New Forest, and exuded a kind of heavy Gothic gloom. He ushered us into his dismal parlour where I looked around hopefully for booze, but had to settle for a very nasty cup of Nescafé. After that we got down to business, looking for suitable subjects for exorcism. Father (drink, drugs and flagellation) and my Aunt Olivia – (drink, drugs and black lesbians) both came under suspicion, but Macnab didn't think they were really the answer.

'Have you lost any children?' he asked.

'Yes,' I said. 'There was a boy who miscarried at four months – we were going to call him William, after his grandfather.'

'Ah!' cried Macnab with great satisfaction. 'I think we've got it! It's little Willy who's never been baptised, and the poor little soul is wandering around the earth waiting to be taken up to heaven. Every now and then he gives you a sharp dig in the stomach just to remind you he's still here!'

After that we all knelt on the floor and prayed together – poor Shura looking extremely embarrassed – and Dr Macnab got down to the nitty-gritty. First a small donation was in order, and then he would arrange for little Willy to be exorcised at a special mass in Westminster Cathedral, conducted by his friend Father Benedict. I would also take my family tree with me and lay it on the altar, as he thought my father and my aunt could both do with a bit of help, judging by what he'd heard of them.

Well, I thought, why not? Compared to lying swathed in yeti fur under a pile of frozen peas or pouring half a pint of black coffee up my backside every morning, an exorcism in Westminster Cathedral sounded a reasonably dignified procedure.

Father Benedict opened the door of his presbytery looking a bit fraught. 'Come in, come in! I'll be with you in a minute, but I've got a load of surplices in the washing-machine – wait just a jiffy while I put them in the dryer.'

After I'd sat around for a bit in the parlour reading about missionaries in the Amazon rain forests, he came beetling back and gave me the bad news: before I could attend Mass and take communion he'd have to hear my confession. My heart sank. It was a good forty years since my last confession, and those years had not been exactly wasted. By the time I'd finished the surplices were ready for ironing and – presumably – I was now pure enough to take communion.

I had hoped for a rather grand and dramatic experience in the cathedral itself, but sadly enough it took place in a small private chapel. My ancestors were duly laid on the altar, Mass was said for a Special Intention and little Willy's soul ascended to heaven – where, Father Benedict explained, my mother would be happily waiting to receive him.

After another donation of £50 to the good Father we adjourned in great spirits to the pub next door and ordered large whiskies and a ploughman's lunch.

I've always found it odd that you're supposed to fast before partaking of the body of Christ in communion, but it's all right to send an enormous breakfast hurtling down on top of him afterwards.

I would love to be able to say that a miraculous cure was effected as a result of all this, but nothing changed. It wasn't until one icy day next February, when I was crossing the extraordinarily dangerous junction of Redcliffe Gardens with the Fulham Road that fate finally took pity on me. A lorry came belting round the corner and as I ran in panic I slipped on the icy surface and went tip over arse on to the tarmac. I shall never be quite sure what happened next – maybe something quite simple, like a trapped nerve in my back being released – but the evil ancestor flew out of my gullet, little Willy went to heaven and Miasma departed, never to return.

Chapter Twelve

After years of pain, I now felt well enough to work again. I had done a lot of food-writing over the years, and now was lucky enough to land a really good job with the prestigious French guide Gault et Millau, writing up restaurants in London and New York.

Instead of bohemianism at The Chelsea, I now found myself in a posh Fifth Avenue hotel where I soon learned to relish the self-indulgent life of well-heeled Americans; amazing breakfasts, alcoholic brunches and the pleasures of room service – oysters and champagne in bed while watching a wet T-shirt contest on *Midnight Blue*.

The work was fairly rigorous, and we normally did two or even three ethnic restaurants a day, dashing between Thai and Tibetan during the lunch hour and ending up at night at a Kosher Chinese in the garment district where they got round the laws by serving such revolting substances as 'Fo-nee Shrimp', made of bean–curd.

The arrival of our employers, Monsieur and Madame Millau, was eagerly awaited. They turned out to be a typically 'bon bourgeois' couple of rigid respectability, which made what happened on our first night together even more surprising.

After a very grand dinner at Lutèce, with the staff bowing and scraping, we found ourselves in a taxi – heading, I thought, for home. But Millau had other ideas. 'Now we shall go to Plato's Retreat,' he announced. 'I want you to do a piece on it.'

Plato's Retreat? Wasn't that a sort of orgy club where people made love in public? After a week of eating two or three meals a day I was in no shape to take my clothes off, not that I wanted to, and certainly not in the company of Monsieur and Madame Millau.

'Don't worry,' he said. 'It is *très amusant*, and you need only watch!'

The first thing that surprised me, when we finally drew up outside the red door, was the row of hookers lined up outside. Apparently single men are not allowed in the club, and a lot of them even have to resort to taking their wives.

We went in fully clothed, and – surprise, surprise! – many others were too, except for a few men who were wearing white towels tucked around their waists like babies' nappies. Where were the writhing bodies, the bouncing boobs? At first all we could see were two fat men in nappies playing billiards. I advanced nervously, looking for the action, and finally spotted a naked girl throwing herself around on the dance floor. Sinister ladies in black leather and suspenders, known as Dominatrixes, were strutting their stuff on the sidelines, acting as house cheerleaders, but there was a notable lack of abandon.

It was in fact a rather suburban scene – no gays, no blacks, but nice respectable couples on their night out. A girl would feel safer here than on 42nd Street.

By now I was desperately looking around for a drink, and spotted a sort of country-club buffet, with creamed chicken, tuna salad and, thank God, large punch bowls. Unfortunately these turned out to contain only fruit juice. Now I knew why so many men were wearing loin cloths – it was the only place they had to stash a hip flask.

I moved on, lured by the scented steam rising from a tented Roman swimming-pool. Sex at last! Someone was actually getting laid in the shallow end, with an ecstatic smile on her face, but no one was swimming. A lifeguard dressed as a gladiator, who must have had one of the city's cushiest sinecures, was squatting on the edge of the pool chewing gum.

'Have you ever had to rescue somebody?' I asked.

The guard shifted his wad to the other cheek. 'Who? Me? Jump in there? Listen, lady, if they was drowning you wouldn't get me into *that* water!'

From there I went to investigate the movie rooms, one of which was showing very unattractive people doing you-know-what, the other an old Peter Sellers movie which seemed to be rather more popular.

Finally I came to it – the holy of holies, the inner sanctum known as the Mattress Room. This is where the action is, the place where your uptight executive finally sheds his inhibitions along with his blue dacron two-piece. Stern notices line the entrance. 'Remove your clothes!' 'Respect your neighbour!' 'Take no food into the Mattress Room!' Anyone with kinky ideas about Mars bars might as well forget them.

Huddled round the door stood a shifty-looking group of fully-clothed punters trying to cop a look without actually going in. They were eyed with disapproval and moved on. It is easier to get into the Ritz without a tie than into the Mattress Room with your trousers on. Luckily a few strategically placed peep-holes are let into the walls – a kind of X-rated version of What The Butler Saw.

I had never seen other people making love, so my first glimpse of sixty-odd couples all enthusiastically bonking came as a bit of a shock. But it was amazing how soon I got used to it. Quite frankly it was a bit boring – they lay, cheek by jowl (or occasionally jowl by cheek) like so many battery chickens. The missionary position seemed to be top favourite, although an occasional joyous flurry of mixed-up limbs showed where neighbours were not being respected. The girls were mainly attractive, the men rather less so and wearing a look of grim determination, having blown fifty dollars on doing what they could have done at home in front of the telly for free.

After midnight things hotted up a bit on the dance floor. The DJ put on some country and western music, and everybody shed their clothes, set to partners and do-si-doed. If you've never seen a naked square dance, pardner, you ain't seen nuttin'!

It was the club's fifth anniversary, so a birthday cake was borne in, carried aloft by naked ladies and sprouting five chocolate phalluses. The Millaus wanted to do more research but by now my husband was in deep conversation with a very attractive Chinese girl who had just shed her cheongsam, so I thought it was time to leave.

This was my last assignment in New York and though I missed the glamour and luxury I had to admit there had been certain drawbacks – like putting on half a stone. I felt in need of a complete change, and started to skim through the jobs columns in the local papers. One day I saw an ad in the *Chelsea News* – 'Cook wanted for the Royal Court Theatre'.

I had sworn never to work in a restaurant again, but the lure of the stage, let alone the stove, was too great – I could feel my fingers itching for a wooden spoon. My spirits fell when I saw the 'kitchen' – a sink and two electric rings in the circle bar. The only oven was hidden away downstairs in a cubby hole behind the stalls, and you had to carry your food through the foyer to get to it. My job was to feed the actors and staff during rehearsals, and the pay worked out at slightly less than £2 an hour. Nevertheless it turned out to be the nicest job I'd ever had.

Monday, 15 August 1977. My first day at the Royal Court. Cammy and I wheeled a huge container of chilli con carne down the King's Road in my shopping trolley, and we got started. I may not be much of a gourmet cook, but at least I'm a fast one. As I brewed coffee, boiled rice for the chilli, made salads and fought my way through the foyer with trays of apple crumble I could see the washer-up's mouth hanging open in disbelief. 'You've never seen my mother in action before, have you?' said Cammy proudly.

Luckily it wasn't a big rush – just the cast of *Once a Catholic*, plus the staff, who were very friendly and kept wandering in for a chat and a coffee. I thought it a wonderful job, especially as I could watch rehearsals in the afternoon.

I had been stage-struck ever since I was at RADA, but was also pathologically gun-shy, which kept me away from an awful lot of plays apart the classics. I don't think I've ever seen a gun in real life, but it's amazing how people start waving them around as soon as they get on stage. Visits to plays had to be prefaced by embarrassing conversations with the front of house manager. 'I'm – er – thinking of taking my aged mother to your play. She's a bit gun-shy, poor old dear – the Blitz, you know! Can you tell me if your production features any bombs, explosions or gun shots? I have to ask because even Shakespeare isn't safe nowadays, is he?' Now, at the Court, I could watch rehearsals of well-vetted plays at my leisure, without the awful pitfalls involved in actually going to the theatre.

Thursday, 18 August. The atmosphere here is remorselessly left-wing, and I sometimes wonder what the hell a rather wet Tory like me is doing in this temple to street cred and trade unionism. I am trying hard to conceal my upper-class origins, and practise saying 'off' instead of 'orf', but I'm not sure if I'm fooling them. Actually they like my food so much that they probably don't care.

Harriet, the publicity manager, has street cred to a quite alarming degree. She wears faded jeans and no make-up, lives in a fashionably unfashionable part of north London and has two children called Sky and Blue. Nothing escapes her beady eye. If a bit of pan-scourer unravels and ends up in the stew it'll always be Harriet who finds it and stalks across the room holding it out at arm's length.

I am also rather frightened of Ann Jenkins, the general manager, an extremely competent lady who wears red trouser suits with matching glasses. Most of the men are very jolly, ranging from John Aitken the house manager, who is a delight and an endless source of bitchy gossip, to the 'lads' – Jack, Duncan and Robin – who work in the lighting box in a permanent haze of tobacco smoke and beer fumes.

Tuesday, 4 October. Came in expecting to cater for twelve and was suddenly swamped by the entire cast of *The Good Woman of Szechuan*, extras and all. In a panic rushed to Sainsbury's, bought fifty chicken pieces, some packets of country stuffing and a few tins of pineapple, combined them all in a couple of roasting tins and rushed down to the oven. A huge success! Ann Jenkins was most impressed. 'The thing about you and me, Joan,' she said, 'is that we are both pros!' I positively glowed with pleasure. I wonder if it would work with pork chops?

* *

Monday, 2 January 1978. First day of rehearsal for *Laughter*. I had hoped for some nice, light-hearted comedy but halfway through getting my Irish stew with dumplings together I heard fearful screams coming from the theatre below. These continued at regular intervals throughout the morning, and a quick visit to the circle confirmed my worst fears. Far from being a comedy, the first act of *Laughter* was set in the Tsar's torture chamber, and featured a prisoner, stage right, transfixed on a pike. 'Does it get any funnier?' I asked the director, Charles Marowitz. 'Hardly,' he said giving me a scathing look. 'The second half is set in Dachau.'

Later I had a big row with the ASM because I wouldn't give him two dumplings. He practically burst into tears and called me a mean bitch, but why should he have two when everybody else only has one?

Tuesday, 6 December 1978. Plays here seem unremittingly gloomy of late. Take *Wheelchair Willy* – 'Rape, unemployment, poverty, violence and sexual depravity, handicapped Willy's home life is far from idyllic', as the programme notes have it.

Friday, 3 May 1979. More concentration camps! Tom Bell and Ian McKellan are doing a play called *Bent*. Bell is a great disappointment – having only seen the great, bony face shot from below in dramatically-lit films, I was not prepared for a small meek-looking fellow in wire spectacles. McKellan, on the other hand, is gorgeous.

I was cooking bangers in my stalls cubbyhole when I became aware of a presence looming behind me, and was thrilled to find it was McKellan. I had always fancied him, in spite of his being gay. 'I like my sausages burnt,' he said, peering into the frying pan. 'Practically incinerated, if you can manage it!' I obliged with some really carbonised objects with nice round crispy bits bursting out at the ends.

After lunch I watched him with Tom Bell doing their famous love scene in Dachau where they make love verbally across the full length of the stage, without touching each other, and felt proud to think that it was my sausages that were fuelling their ardour.

I worked at the Royal Court for two very happy years, and only left because I found I needed more time for my writing. Camilla had come across my old wartime diaries in a trunk in the attic. She had been riveted by them – though enraged that I had had such a good time when young: better than she had, in fact – and convinced me that I must edit and publish them. So I had a farewell party in the bar and got very sloshed with the staff, who seemed genuinely sorry to see me go. The best moment came at the end when Harriet – the street-cred queen – kissed me goodbye. 'I'll say something for you, Joan,' she said, 'you're a Royal Court person *through* and *through*!' I felt it was the best compliment anyone had ever paid me, even if undeserved.

Chapter Thirteen

𝒩 Did I think writing was going to be easy? I must have
been mad. Compared with writing, cooking meals for
fifty people a day had been a doddle.

It was amazing how many other things I could think of to
do just to avoid the typewriter. I turned out drawers and
cupboards, went to films in the afternoon, planned elaborate
dinner parties and revamped my entire wardrobe. No one,
unfortunately, has yet invented the equivalent of a literary
laxative that deals with writer's block. When I finally got down
to it, I found it a lonely business, and to make matters worse
Camilla had just moved out of the basement in Wellington
Square, and found herself a flat with a studio, where she could
sculpt. My lodger Kerry had left for Canada, and I began to
look around desperately for a new lodger.

I was at a New Year's Eve party of Jay Landesman's in Soho
in 1981 when I first saw Salman. He was wearing a black leather
jacket over a white T-shirt with LOVE printed on it, tight
trousers and winkle picker shoes. He loped towards me, moving
like an antelope shot in slow motion, and I was aware of golden
skin, pouting, mulberry-stained lips, and dark mournful eyes
full of self-mockery, that looked up coyly from under sweeping
lashes. All this oriental splendour was topped by an enormous

cornucopia of glossy pomaded hair, rising up straight and shiny like a black helmet. He introduced himself as a friend of Cammy's, and told me he was looking for a room.

According to my daughter he was a very sweet, gentle person who took her out to tea at the Patisserie Valerie. He worked at the ICA and wrote poetry in his spare time. I thought he would be ideal – good manners, a steady job and sufficiently eccentric to fit into our household – and I took him in without further thought, little knowing what sorrow he would one day cause me.

In no time, Sal – as he liked to be called – had transformed my rather drab top room into an exotic haven, scented with sandalwood and hung with Indian carpets. There were expensive art books on the shelves, and wreaths of paper roses round the mirror. He particularly loved the view from his window, looking out over a garden full of trees.

On his first morning he pranced down to the kitchen in a yellow silk dressing-gown, carrying a bowl of multi-coloured vitamin pills – his breakfast – and then retired for a lengthy session in the bathroom. There was, it seemed, no question of his actually having a bath – immersion in water terrified him because of what it might do to his hair. But there was plenty of massaging with fragrant oils and rubbing down with friction gloves, followed by the final brushing up and lacquering of his elaborate coiffure.

Over the first few days he told me that he was twenty-eight – untrue: he was twenty-one – and that his family were very grand and lived in a palace in India – untrue again: his father was a respectable academic living in London. He also told me about his beautiful younger sister who had run away with a lover and was the black sheep of the family, but he seemed rather vague as to her whereabouts. Surprisingly, he boasted about all the girlfriends who were madly in love with him, whereas to me he seemed quite obviously gay.

On the following Saturday morning he went out early, leaving a sealed yellow envelope for me on the kitchen table. It was tied up with pink ribbon, and on the front he had drawn a naked faun playing the flute. The margin was illuminated in red ink with the words pain, perversity, torment, madness, ecstasy, delirium and death! Inside was the rent.

By now I was finding Sal thoroughly endearing, albeit a shocking liar. He always seemed happy, and was always rushing out to parties and openings. On the rare occasions when he stayed at home he sat on the sofa watching telly, swathed in a rather tatty ermine cloak with only the tip of his nose and the topmost plume of his hair showing. His favourite viewing was *Brideshead Revisited*.

I was not to realise until much later that this happy exterior was the biggest lie of all. Upstairs in his room, unbeknown to us, Sal was writing:

A new month, a new home. I cringe from so much newness, white pages waiting to be scarred by my contaminated ink. My writing is like a private realm.

I live in a vacuum, an observer, never engaged. I inhabit my own zonked-out zombie realm. Nothing overwhelms me, – a walking freaked-out wreck who *looks* good but is dead inside. My smiles hide the utter disintegration within.

To fill my voids I have become Café society's darling child, everybody's golden dream-boy. It must be true, they tell me so – so why do I wish to die?

I don't really want to take my life but the despair is so intense, so recurrent that I'm halfway there already. Like a parasite that feeds on itself, I am both Prometheus and the eagle, wrenching out my heart and asking my own pardon. Like Salome I dance my dance of death, decapitate myself and present myself with my own head – huge eyes, gaping mouth. A cry in the dark, a scream – save me! Mother, where are you? Living frightens me. They say drowning is a sublime way to go.

Another aspect of life that frightened Sal was his homo-sexuality, which he found somehow degrading. Gay pubs turned him to a shaking jelly.

Then one day I introduced him in the French Pub to Francis Bacon, and through him to R.F., a successful West End art dealer who became his lover.

*

What am I doing in this homosexual mayhem, stretched out like a beast in four-posted splendour lit by the maverick flame of our penultimate candle? R.F. is next door taking out his contact lenses. He's hot, a pure boy's peril, the ultimate corruptor of young acolytes.

What am I doing with this man of forty-five? When he drinks his cheeks flush and the wine dribbles from the corner of his mouth. When I sleep with him I emerge parched, barren and dizzy from his clutches. This is not love, not truth, just rotting physicality.

I try to pretend I am doing it for experience and edification – I offer you my sweetness, you offer me your culture. But I suppose I am just what they call an Art Tart. Afterwards I cry and wash manically, trying to expiate, to purify myself.

For months he felt himself unable to visit his parents, knowing how much they disapproved of him, everything from his appearance to his way of life. He had always been plagued by asthma, but now it became worse and he found himself unable to write.

I'm a complete wastrel, I do nothing! Here I sit, saturnine, self-conscious, an elegant, silent prick, invisibly frothing at the mouth. I look at the empty page and realise what an unproductive arsehole I've become, lazy, hazy and wallowing in self-indulgence. What a bore I am with my death wish, my puerile little idiosyncracies. I am lost and I suppose I want to be. I must do, because in a way I really delight in this situation like some clapped-out failed romantic. I posture and mouth clichés – Die young! Live to excess! Create a legend! Never compromise! Curse Philistinism!

Shut your trap, epileptic!

Shortly after wrting this he split from R.F. and went back to being a normal, fun-loving boy, with Cammy as his willing accomplice.

Bored with coffee, so drank vodka for breakfast. So happy now: I want *everything*. Cammy is beautiful, I really love her. Tonight she cooked up a storm turning the kitchen into a battleground. She looks like an urchin in a Victorian work-house. Afterwards snuggled, and ate chocolate in front of a bad Sixties movie. Then upstairs to fold myself into my sheets and dream of Montezuma and a golden world.

Cammy in foul mood because she feels lonely, so take her to smart Art Tart's party. Watch her sticking her little stubby fingers into the mushroom dip while chatting up some blond prat from Calnaghis. Afterwards to Gaz's Rockin' Blues. R.F. there and cut me dead. I am all tarted up in my best black leather, scrubbed and fragrant. C. says I look like a cross between a pixie and a B-movie vampire. I dance like a maniac and people gaze with awe and contempt at this six-foot prancing Eastern beauty.

Sal's beauty – or lack of it – was one of his principal obsessions:

Looking at myself in the mirror I realise what a struggle it is to attain beauty. So much time, worry and care! I have little natural beauty. It is all nurtured and cultivated and when it slips through my fingers my mind too begins to collapse. It is the one surety that I can cling to, but I exhaust myself in keeping it up!

A big blow to his vanity came when he walked out in front of a taxi, breaking his nose and fracturing a bone in his leg. It was the nose that upset him the most, and some desperate scribbling followed. 'My nose, my nose, my nose! When will the swelling go? How long will it take to assume its former shape? Oh please, please, please go! I who was once so beautiful – (oh rancid vanity) – all I have now is one profile!'

However, his stay in hospital produced one unexpected bonus – a prescription for a powerful pain-killer called DF118. For weeks afterwards he went back to the doctor for repeat prescriptions, taking a few, and, unknown to me, hoarding the rest. If I asked for one to relieve a headache he would react like a miser whose gold was threatened.

Convinced he was still in pain, we took him down to the cottage to recuperate. He had never been to the country before, and the locals eyed him with dismay. The first time he walked into our local, The Russell Arms, dressed in black leather with his oiled cockscomb rampant, all conversation was brought to a standstill.

After this episode he preferred to lurk in the safety of the garden. We were all sunbathing, but Sal stayed well wrapped up in the shade of the apple tree, afraid for his complexion. A visit to our local swimming-pool was even less successful. Sal sat on the edge looking gloomily at the water, that dangerous element which could turn his crowning glory into an untrendy tangle of curls.

I left out the visitors book for him to write in, but he declined. Later, when I went to the loo, I saw the words 'Salman, Adonis Perversus Rex sat here!'

Somehow I don't think Sal was a cottage person.

One happy result of his break with R.F. was that he felt free again to visit the father he so loved and feared:

My father leaves for New York tomorrow. Oh how I'll miss him! He thinks I'm an ungrateful wretch, he disapproves of my hair, my clothes, my life-style, but I really love him. When he gets moody I pull his cheeks and kiss him. His hair is such a beautiful shade of silver grey. We had tea together today. Afterwards, I went into the bathroom and suddenly saw my face as he must see it, ugly and depraved. I cried and cried.

I still think he could have been saved if, in the spring of 1983, he had not met James McEwan. That was when the final countdown began that was to cost so many lives.

James was everything Sal had dreamed of – a young friend of his own age, aristocratic and wild, happy and generous. The whole set-up appealed to Sal's innate snobbery, like *Brideshead Revisited* come to life; the great house in Scotland, the new young friend and even a beautiful and deeply Catholic mother.

During that long, hot summer, Sal spent much of his time up in Scotland with James, trying to cure him of his heroin addiction, but also enjoying the unfamiliar pleasures of having fun with a big family. In particular, James's sister, the lovely Katie, became an intimate friend.

'James and I are tired of our bedrooms,' he wrote. 'We are camping out in the great ballroom!'

He came back to London at the beginning of June, leaving James still on heroin, crazed and wild.

On 23 June James got up early and washed his hair. Then he went upstairs to the room where Sal had been sleeping during his recent stay. He locked the door, lay down on the bed, wedged a shotgun between his legs, reached down and pulled the trigger.

Sal went up to Scotland for the funeral. He said they took music down to the grave and danced around it, defying demons. A few weeks later, he brought Katie down to live with us.

She was twenty-five and a student at the Slade; boyishly slender, short, with dark hair under a beret worn straight over her winged eyebrows, her eyes and mouth big in a small face.

She and Sal huddled together upstairs like babes in the wood, comforting each other. They made a pact that they would always love and look after each other, even when they were old.

Katie, I soon discovered, was anorexic and made the merest pretence of eating her meals. One night I tried to tempt her with roast goose, but she only picked at a few shreds. Later that night I heard a scrabbling noise in the kitchen, and came down to investigate. As I stood on the landing a figure raced past me in the dark, leaving greasy handprints on the banisters. I realised with horror that she had crept down, mad with hunger, to look for the goose carcass in the dustbin. After that I would try to lure her with small portions of something delicate, and always left the room while she ate it as I knew she hated to be watched.

In August she went back to Marchmont, and Sal wrote to her:

To the alluring and dazzling K.!
    Just remember – those demons don't really *exist*, not really, not corporeally – they might float around us in little mists but they are useless, *impotent* without us, like a record without a record player. It is we who conjure *them* up. I know you know I know what I mean! So let's face the shit and spit in the face of death and fate! Life is the farce we must all lead – (Rimbaud's words, not mine). So let's celebrate art, beauty passion and love – but not Dementia.
    Dance, dance, dance!
    I wish you a restful night, and glorious morning.

In September, Katie went on holiday to Africa with two of

her friends. She found she was not getting on too well with them, so one Thursday morning she left the villa and changed all her money at the bank. Then she went down to a nearby beach, known locally as the 'bad beach'.

Her body was found next day washed up on the sand. She was wearing bra and pants, there were bruises and abrasions on her body, and her ear lobes were missing. The local police refused to investigate.

Sal showed little or no emotion; he seemed in shock. During the week before her funeral, he went up to Marchmont with a group of her young friends. It was an extraordinary week, filled with a desperate need to exorcise demons and celebrate the continuing normality of life. They danced, played football, climbed trees and picked mushrooms. Then they followed the coffin up a steep hill, the pipers going before playing 'The Flowers of the Forest'.

Between September and Christmas, Sal, like a cancer patient enjoying a remission, became almost joyous. There was no more doom-laden scribbling. It was almost as if his two best friends had died instead of him.

He also had a new friend called Caroline, a girl he had met at the funeral. 'Not just a *double*-barrelled surname,' he boasted gleefully, 'but *triple*-barrelled!' She was not a lover, as the others had been, but she helped to keep him sane, and he would sometimes visit her in Scotland.

Two weeks before Christmas, I came home to find the whole house transformed into an Aladdin's Cave. Every inch was hung with balloons, wreathes of evergreen, and glistening strands of silver foil and tinsel. In front of the fireplace was Sal, doing a little triumphal dance. 'This is going to be the best Christmas of my life,' he said. 'I feel it in my bones!'

It was going to be the first Christmas we had ever spent together, as over the last two years he had always slipped abroad to avoid it. He was also looking forward with great excitement to spending New Year in Scotland with Caroline and her family.

On Saturday 17 December, the busiest day for shoppers, the IRA exploded a bomb just outside Harrods.

We heard the news two days later, while we were dressing to go out to dinner. Sal, in great spirits, was getting ready for his annual ICA party at the Mermaid Theatre. On our way down we looked in on the kitchen, meaning to turn out the lights, and saw Sal standing by the sink in his black and white party clothes, holding the *Evening Standard* in his hands. He looked like someone who had run into a stone wall. He held out the paper to us and we saw on the front page a smiling face that we recognised – it was Caroline, 'civilian victim of the Harrods bomb outrage'.

I moved towards him, but he backed away as if he were a leper. 'Don't touch me,' he said. 'I don't think I'm safe to know.'

The Mermaid Theatre at Puddle Dock looks out on the river and Blackfriars Bridge. Once there, Sal danced incessantly, manically. Soon after midnight he asked, or rather begged, his friend Jonathan to come home with him, but Jonathan had another party to go to. 'You will regret this,' Sal said.

The next day passed peacefully, and Sal's absence aroused no fear in us. He often stayed with friends. It was only when the ICA rang up on Wednesday morning to say he had not turned up for work that I felt the first stab of fear. Shura rang the police, but they were very offhand. Young boys, they said, were always going off and disappearing for days – what was the panic?

By Thursday, we were really worried, and got on to a Chief Inspector, who promised to do what he could. The phone rang at four in the morning – something had come up on the computer, a body washed ashore on the Isle of Dogs.

'It's a boy,' the Inspector said, 'with dark curly hair.' For a moment my heart leapt, until I remembered why Sal had been so frightened of water. 'What was he wearing?' we asked.

'Tight black trousers, pointed shoes and a white T-shirt with LOVE printed on it.'

The next day Shura went to the morgue and our final doubts were dispelled. In spite of the efforts of the morticians Sal's face was swollen and almost ugly, his mouth slightly agape. The hair was a mass of curls.

It was two days before Christmas, and his presents were already under the tree. By Christmas morning we were unable to bear the house a moment longer. Luckily John and Jane Stonehouse were kind enough to take us in for Christmas and we went over carrying huge quantities of food and wine, our eyes still swollen with tears.

Sal's father was in hospital, too ill to be told, and when we broke the news to his mother, she refused to believe it because, she said, he had always been frightened of water.

When his father had recovered, his parents came to collect his few personal possessions. While Shura kept them talking in the sitting-room, I rushed upstairs to hide anything incriminating. Gay magazines were kicked under the bed. On the desk was a book of poetry open at Rilkes 'Death of a Young Poet'. I closed it. The top drawer of the chest contained a dozen bottles labelled DF118, each containing ten pills. Lying neatly on top of them was a piece of paper with careful instructions: 'DF118 - 100 × 25 mgs. Two plastic bags three foot in length, eighteen inches wide. Two or three elastic bands around the neck. Take drugs five minutes before fixing bag.'

I tore up the note and hid the pills in the room next door. In the next drawer, I spotted a jumbo-size Toblerone bar, Sal's favourite late night snack, and mine too. It felt suspiciously heavy. Ripping it open I discovered a small vibrator bought by Sal in a drunken moment from Ann Summers Sex Shop. His parents were already coming upstairs, so I stuffed it under my jacket.

When his mother saw how clean and beautiful his room was, she cried for the first time, and I put my arms around her to comfort her, one arm a bit rigid in an effort to keep the incriminating vibrator from falling to the floor.

Afterwards, over tea, I remembered Sal's naughty sister Zara, the black sheep of the family. 'Have you broken the news yet to his sister?' I asked.

'What sister? Sal never had a sister,' they said.

The father left, taking all Sal's diaries – all, that is, but the white one, which was at the back of a cupboard, and one other which had been found washed up at the water's edge with our address in it.

It was black and soggy, smelling of decay. The red ink inside had run into illegible blotches, but the newspaper cutting stuck on the front cover was still legible: Sir James McEwan, aged twenty-three, had died at his home in Scotland of gun-shot wounds. There were no suspicious circumstances.

My final task, after stripping and tidying his room, was to open any mail that had accumulated since his death. One envelope contained a Christmas card from his father. He said how upset he was that Sal thought him stingy in his love towards him and that Sal could have no idea how much he had suffered for him and loved him, from a small boy to a grown-up. He went on to say how much both he and Sal's mother had suffered through their separation from him, and how much they wished he could have tried to meet them at least half-way. He ended sadly and ironically with the wish that God would guide him through his tumultuous life, and with best wishes for a happy New Year with peace, contentment and freedom from anguish.

It was the letter he had always been waiting and hoping for. Written two days before his death, it arrived too late.

Three months later, I had an extraordinary experience. I was consulting a clairvoyant about my health, and was sitting in a bright sunny room on a chintz sofa with no thought of Sal in my mind. Suddenly the medium, who had been generalising rather vaguely, broke off and started staring at a spot on the wall.

'I don't want to upset you,' she said, 'but there's a young man here who died recently. He's standing just over there behind the sofa. What an extraordinary face he has – so open and clear-eyed. He sends you lots of love but what he would really like to do is run across the room and hug you in a warm, tight embrace. He asks you to accept his apologies for the appalling *timing* of what he did, and all the mess he left behind for you to clear up. There is a young male friend standing next to him who also died. He is laughing and saying that they still have a lot of pranks together, but have sobered up quite a bit. After death you can either go forward or back to the age that suits you best. So he is now twenty-eight, the age he always wanted to be. He says you want to ask him a question.'

'What happened? Why did he do it?'

'He says he had a temporary blackout and his head went into a flat spin. His whole life had been a form of Russian roulette: he thought all the time about death, but strangely enough, after all this planning, when it happened it was almost an accident – suddenly all the right conditions came about, and he jumped. After his head went under the water, he was aware for about three to five seconds of what was happening, but after that he was above his body, out of himself. He watched himself struggling as if in a dream but felt completely calm. He knew he had done wrong but there was no pain or fear in those last moments.

'He asks your forgiveness for being such a pain, being so bloody-minded and telling you so many fibs. It was what he calls a kind of "naughty unhappiness". He was a person who never wanted to be born and he was deeply unhappy for most of his life and made others unhappy too. He says to tell you that now he understands himself, and is at peace.'

My darling Sal, I wish you a restful night and a glorious morning.

Chapter Fourteen

I am not sure to what extent these tragedies affected my decision, but about a year later I decided it was time to leave Wellington Square. I wanted a new beginning, a new house without bad memories. I had no idea what I was in for.

For a start there is the trauma of selling your old home. Every day – in case the estate agent rings – you have to have an early bath, put on your most respectable clothes and clean and tidy everything in a way normally reserved for special occasions. Then, in they come – a horde of seemingly hostile and suspicious strangers who all think the price is too high. Why do they look with such scorn at your grotty but dearly loved furniture, why has the cat always just been sick on the stairs?

We finally sold it, and the moving out process began. I felt like a murderer as I emptied out old cupboards and chucked away their contents, throwing away the happy years of youth and bad behaviour to move into a house where I would probably die. The new owners were planning to gut the place and spend a fortune renovating it.

As I walked through the house for the last time, I realised with a pang of nostalgia that there was hardly a single inch of it where someone, at some time, had not made love.

Of course it *did* have its disadvantages: no central heating, no garden, damp and dry rot. By contrast our new modern house, with its huge picture windows and patio garden, is positively Hollywood, but still I miss Wellington Square.

We are now on the Fulham Road, known to *Tatler* readers as 'Funset Strip' – more sunset than funset down our end, with everything I need to see me out within 300 yards of my front door: the hospital, the undertakers, the church where I was baptised and the Brompton Cemetery where I shall doubtless be buried. The cats love the garden and prowl around it, marking their territory, howling at invisible foes over the wall. It is a lazy person's garden, full of ivies and evergreens, apart from some rather hideous pink hydrangeas which I haven't the heart to cut down.

For the first couple of months we put up with wall-to-wall brown hessian and a cramped kitchen, but sooner or later the builders and decorators had to move in and a new nightmare began.

Downstairs in the kitchen, four Rastas worked in a permanent haze of ganja smoke which rose in aromatic waves to the little room upstairs where we sat hunched on boxes over our morning Nescafé, heated up on a small electric ring.

After breakfast, I would go downstairs to interfere with the painters, who groaned when they saw me approaching. No, I didn't want everything in magnolia, thank you, I preferred to mix my own colours. Into the pail went a spot of mushroom, a dash of catkin and a smidgeon of whale grey, finally ending up with the sort of indeterminate beige that I could easily have got from a Dulux colour chart.

Meanwhile, in the hall, an orange-haired punk and his cowed bondage-slave girlfriend were laying ceramic tiles, and threatening to take them up with a pick axe if our cheque was a day late. Would the misery never end?

By Christmas, however, we were finally straight and I began to settle down, like a caddis-worm that has finally succeeded in making itself a new shell.

Another good point about the new house was its proximity to Cammy, who was still working as a sculptor, and living just around the corner in Edith Grove. We were now within a fast five-minute trot of each other – I could go round there to dump on her whenever I was feeling low, and she could nip over to have a coffee, read my Sunday papers and borrow a fiver.

Clare was still living in Tuscany, but brown rice, miso soup and strangling chickens was now a thing of the past. Instead, much to my relief, her husband had gone into computer software, and had an office in Florence and another in the States. Now they could actually buy the farmhouse instead of renting it, and were talking about putting in a new kitchen and a swimming pool. I couldn't have been more pleased.

Things were also going well on the work front, for with the builders out of the way, I could finally start to write again, working on my third book of autobiography. My last book about life in the WAAF was still selling well, although my publishers got the occasional rude letter starting 'This woman Wyndham is a disgrace to her uniform!'

One day my old friend Pandora talked me into going to a WAAF reunion. We took one look at a roomful of blue rinses and fled to the Victory Bar, where I was accosted by a fierce-looking ex-sergeant in her seventies.

'Oh, it's *you*, Wyndham!' she cried, spotting my badge. 'The one who used to *read* on watch. Put Wyndham on a quiet station, we used to say, she *reads*!' I suppose a combination of Proust and myopia might have sent a few brave boys into the drink, but on the whole I think I managed to muddle through.

Nowadays, my tastes in literature are far less highbrow – mostly detective stories bought for 60p at car boot sales or American crime novels from a wonderful shop called Murder One, with titles like *Kiss Your Ass Goodbye*. I think one's tastes in general deteriorate as one grows older, as I also have a passion for whisky, cigarettes, Mars Bars, *Blind Date* and Princess Di.

Having cooked all my life, I now detest it, and my favourite snack is last night's cold Indian take-away eaten straight from the fridge, standing up and preferably with the fingers, or the top two spoonfuls from a tin of cold baked beans.

As for writing, I find I can only do it in odd bursts – in fact the various maneouvres I've employed to avoid writing this book have succeeded in giving me quite a full and interesting life.

My pet hate is that lady novelist in the *Sunday Times'* 'A Life in the Day of' who jumps out of bed at six-thirty, eats a bowl of muesli with a glass of hot water, and goes for a brisk canter round Hyde Park before arriving at her desk on the stroke of ten, all smug and glowing.

Why can't someone write something truthful, like 'Woke late

with a dreadful hangover, staggered downstairs for black coffee and a fag and spent the rest of the day alternately reaching for the bottle and avoiding the word processor'?

I sometimes wonder if I only write books for the sheer pleasure I get from taking part in TV and radio interviews. Being married to a gregarious husband with a well-deserved reputation as a raconteur, I find it sheer bliss to be asked lots of personal questions, and to be able to rabbit on about myself endlessly without fear of interruption.

In November 1989 the dice landed me on yet another snake – one of those very long and evil-looking ones that send you straight down to the bottom of the board. I had suspected for some months that I had a rather embarrassing complaint – well, piles actually – so I went into the Westminster for a minor op. When I came round I found the specialist sitting beside my bed with that reassuring smile that usually means they are about to tell you something extremely nasty. I had, it seemed, a malignant tumour – not a huge and life-threatening one, but a small and ultimately dangerous growth in an unfortunate place. Four to five months of radio- and chemo-therapy, he said, might possibly cure it, but otherwise it was major surgery and a colostomy bag.

I went in for my first session of radio-therapy filled with direst forebodings, but everything was done to reassure me. As I lay on the table with the dreaded machine beneath me a nurse switched on Vivaldi, and a large metal screen rose slowly into the air and positioned itself over my head. It was covered with cut-out pictures of gambolling lambs, Alpine meadows and the Blue Grotto in Capri, all designed to keep my mind off the fact that millions of volts of radio-active energy were frying my backside to a crisp.

This was followed by two weeks of chemo-therapy in a small ward, suspended by a tube in my wrist to a heavy machine which I had to drag behind me every time I wanted a fag or a pee. The nurses could not have been nicer, though I wished they wouldn't say 'Just a little prick coming' when they meant two and a half inches of cold steel straight up your bum and into the muscle.

The other three patients in my ward were all worse off than me, and all heroically patient and uncomplaining. They were in fact so remorselessly nice about everyone and everything that I found conversation extremely difficult – if only they'd moaned about the awful food, bitched about the nurses, criticised the doctors or even just occasionally said 'Bugger'. I found myself looking forward fervently to my husband's six o'clock visit, when we could draw the curtains, have a large whisky and play gin rummy.

Much to the doctors' surprise I came through the chemotherapy without a single twinge of nausea or the loss of a single hair – I was a prize patient.

There was only one alarming after-effect: I discovered I had lost my sense of taste. The thought of going through life with everything tasting like boiled turnips seemed to be a fate worse than death, but after a couple of weeks my sense of taste gradually returned, and soon I was tucking in again with my usual relish.

Three months later, the tumour, thank God, had totally disappeared, though friends still tended to treat me like someone under sentence of death. 'Feeling better, darling? I suppose you're having a little remission!' they would say. The worst letter I had was from someone I hardly knew, who wrote to say she hoped I would be allowed to die with dignity at home.

As for Shura, a confirmed hypochondriac, he must have felt I had somehow stolen his thunder. He went for tests to specialists all over London, but was unable to come up with anything more terminal than 'dandruff of the eyelashes'.

11 October 1990. My sixty-ninth birthday. Old age – how I hate it! All my life I've been thinking of other people as 'old' – I've laughed about it, ignored it and suddenly here it is, squatting on my neck with its bony fingers feeling for my jugular. My head has started to poke forward like a turtle peering from its shell, my front teeth fall out when I sneeze, I pick up the cat instead of my handbag. God, how I wish I was young and thin again!

There are, of course, good days and bad days – on a good day I can feel like a Valkyrie riding into battle, but on the bad ones more like a crushed cockroach. Luckily there are more of the former.

Another worry is my memory, which is getting increasingly unreliable. The other day when someone rang up from the *Tatler* for my address I realised that I didn't know where I lived. 'Hold on a minute,' I said, 'there's someone ringing the bell,' and rushed out to check up on my front door.

In spite of all this, I'm still pretty well-preserved for my age, though this too has its disadvantages. 'You're not *seventy*, are you?' a young man said to me recently at a party. 'I took you for a well-worn fifty-five!' I'd rather be a glamorous seventy than a well-worn fifty-five any day.

Even my cats are getting old – about 150 in cat years, I suppose. They can no longer climb walls to protect their territory and when they jump, with extreme difficulty, on to my lap, they make a noise like Connors serving.

I can remember a time when life was full of 'firsts' – the first man I fancied (John Gielgud in *Hamlet*), the first time I got pissed (the French Pub during the Blitz), and so on. From now on I suppose it will be a succession of 'lasts': the last time you book an adventure holiday up the Amazon, run for a bus, hit a ball, ride a horse or dance all night at a party.

How is it possible to go on pretending everything is OK with only ten or fifteen years to go, and to keep that silly smile on your face when tactless teenagers wish you a happy birthday? I can foresee the worst time of all, when hours will seem too long but years too short. Even more terrible is the thought of your loved ones dying before you, leaving you to face death alone. I was never much good at holding my own hand.

Well, that's enough of these gloomy thoughts – I think I'll go downstairs and have a large whisky.

That was a good idea – I feel better already! After all, there is eternity to look forward to, and as time has always been my enemy, eternity should suit me just fine – provided of course that one spends it in heaven. But as most of my sins have been against myself, caused by laziness, lust, greed and sheer stupidity, rather than malice against others, perhaps they'll let me in.

I haven't got the vaguest idea what heaven will be like, but I know what I should like to find there, if anyone is upstairs listening. Apart from all my friends and loved ones, there would be:

A house full of animals, tame and beautiful;
A game of cards every night;
A nightclub in the basement playing Sixties records, staffed by young and indefatigable dancing robots;
The Aegean Sea at the bottom of my garden;
Treacle pudding.

Well, I could go on for ever, but that will do to be getting on with. In the meantime, for every minute of the day that I am free from pain, either mental or physical, I shall thank God and celebrate life.

With the dark days coming when snakes will outnumber ladders, what better can one do?

M. F. K. Fisher

Long Ago in France

'As beautiful a travel book as you can hope to read.'

Quentin Crewe

In 1929, Mary Frances Kennedy Fisher, young, innocent and
newly married, arrived in Burgundy, and discovered a profusion
of tastes, pastimes and sensuous pleasure in Dijon, France's
gastronomic capital. Picaresque, mouth-watering and crowded
with unforgettable characters, *Long Ago in France* is indeed a feast
of a book, a delightful journey back to a voluptuous, genteel
world, now vanished for ever.

'*Long Ago in France* is a Burgundian feast, robust but exquisitely
delicate, as fresh as the ingredients bought in this morning's
market. Laughter spills over the table. The background music,
naturally, is Josephine Baker singing *J'ai deux amours*. The whole
thing is absolutely delicious.'   *Observer*

'The enveloping glow of a young American couple in love, living
on the cheap in 1920s France, is reminiscent of Hemingway – as
are the lush discoveries of French wine and food . . . Marvellously
evocative.'   *Sunday Times*

'M. F. K. Fisher is a poet of the appetites.'   John Updike

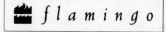

Nick Danziger

Danziger's Travels

Beyond Forbidden Frontiers

'A marvellous account of a truly epic journey . . . Puts him in the forefront of modern travel writers.'　　　　　　　*Mail on Sunday*

Nick Danziger's graphic account of his hair-raising adventures during an eighteen-month journey 'beyond forbidden frontiers' in Asia makes a vivid and unforgettable impact. Travelling in disguise as an itinerant Muslim, his journey on foot and using traditional means of local transport cost him £1,000 in all – exactly one-third of the Winston Churchill travel fellowship he received in London.

After walking and hitch-hiking through southern Turkey and the ayatollahs' Iran, he entred Afghanistan illegally in the wake of a convoy of Chinese weapons and spent two months dodging Russian helicopter gunships with rebel guerrillas. He was the first foreigner to cross from Pakistan into the closed western province of China since the revolution of 1949.

Living and travelling with local people and pitting his wits against officialdom, Danziger broke barriers and crossed boundaries of all kinds. Written with engaging humour and a great zest for life, *Danziger's Travels* is an exceptional travel book in every way, handsomely illustrated with the author's own outstanding photographs and drawings.

'Danziger is the stuff of which legends are made . . . His remarkable story contains some of the most exciting travel writing I have ever read.'　　　　　　　William Dalrymple, *Literary Review*

'Even the most travel-crazy person I know looks unadventurous alongside Nick Danziger.'　　　　　　　*Midweek*

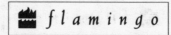 *flamingo*

John David Morley

Pictures from the Water Trade

An Englishman in Japan

'Utterly original and unexpected. The book gives one a totally new and fresh idea of Japanese life – to most of us just about as baffling as life on earth can be. Powerful and picaresque.'   Jan Morris

For several years John David Morley immersed himself in Japanese life, from learning *shodo*, the art of calligraphy, to frequenting the night-time world of the 'water trade', its brothels, nightclubs, transvestite bars and 'pink' cabarets. And he fell in love – deeply, sensually and puzzled to the end.

Written with wonderful panache, wit and delicacy through Morley's alter ego, Boon, *Pictures from the Water Trade* is the entrancing tale of an English writer's journey into the enigma of Japan.

'Arresting and rigorous, *Pictures from the Water Trade* joins the handful of books which display both deep acquaintance and imaginative insight.'   Colin Thubron, *Sunday Telegraph*

'Beguiling, subtle and very funny. One grows into the experience of Japan, making random and often acute discoveries as if for oneself.'   Anthony Thwaite, *Observer*

'Fascinating. Travel literature at its best. Mr Morley is one of those rare travellers who manages to enter the heart of a foreign territory. Rarer still is his ability to take the rest of us along with him.'   Anne Tyler, *New York Times Book Review*

'Vivid, astute and original. He comes closer to the Japanese psyche than most travellers.'   Philip Oakes, *Sunday Times*

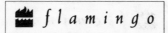

John Williams

Into the Badlands

Travels Through Urban America

'A gazetteer of American *noir*.'   *Daily Telegraph*

In the summer of '89 John Williams donned a baseball cap and
took off for the States to search out the mythical America of the
crime writers, the nation's most astute chroniclers – to find James
Ellroy's LA, Elmore Leonard's sleazy South Beach of Miami,
Sara Paretsky's Chicago. Meeting, among others, George V.
Higgins in Boston and Leonard in Detroit, partying with James
Crumley in Montana and undertaking an unnerving tour of New
York's underbelly with Andrew Vachss, Williams discovers an
urban America at least as disturbing and mesmeric as the popular
fiction of some of his interviewees and gives us an unforgettable,
often hilarious commentary on his own predicament as a
penniless traveller in a string of roachy motels.

'Part travelogue, part interviews, stuffed with anecdotes, critical
asides and astute observation, *Into the Badlands* brings personality
and pleasure into the stuffy and sombre world of literary
commentary . . . a refreshingly vital approach.'   *City Limits*

'I learned a few things. There is vital sociological and moral
comment here too.'   Patricia Highsmith

'An interesting, engaging literary travelogue.'   *Independent*

'A vital mixture of literary criticism, personality profiles and
imaginary geography.'   *New Statesman and Society*

🔥 *fla m i n g o*

Henry Shukman

Sons of the Moon

Travels Among the South American Indians

On a vast plateau high in the Bolivian Andes live 'the sons of the moon', the Aymara. A once-proud pre-Columbian empire that flourished under the gentle light of the moon, Aymara legend tells us that their nation was conquered by the sun-worshipping Incas of Peru, and when the sun rose their fertile land dried up. A few Aymaras remain, scattered in tiny communities; their land, the Altiplano, baked by the equatorial sun and whipped by ferocious winds, is one of the most inhospitable parts of South America, like Patagonia a land of savage, desolate beauty.

The first travel writer to seek out this noble, disappearing race, Henry Shukman describes with rare immediacy the ways of this still-innocent people, taking us to remote outposts and into the hearts of local fiestas, where celebration and violence go hand in hand.

'The Bruce Chatwin *de ses jours*'   *Punch*

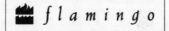

Flamingo

Flamingo is a quality imprint publishing both fiction and non-fiction. Below are some recent titles.

Fiction
- [ ] News From a Foreign Country Came *Alberto Manguel* £4.99
- [ ] The Kitchen God's Wife *Amy Tan* £4.99
- [ ] A Thousand Acres *Jane Smiley* £5.99
- [ ] The Quick *Agnes Rossi* £4.99
- [ ] The Crown of Columbus *Michael Dorris & Louise Erdrich* £5.99
- [ ] The Cat Sanctuary *Patrick Gale* £5.99
- [ ] Dreaming in Cuban *Cristina Garcia* £5.99
- [ ] Mary Swann *Carol Shields* £4.99
- [ ] True Believers *Joseph O'Connor* £5.99
- [ ] Bastard Out of Carolina *Dorothy Allison* £5.99

Non-fiction
- [ ] The Proving Grounds *Benedict Allen* £5.99
- [ ] Long Ago in France *M. F. K. Fisher* £5.99
- [ ] Ford Madox Ford *Alan Judd* £6.99
- [ ] C. S. Lewis *A. N. Wilson* £5.99
- [ ] Into the Badlands *John Williams* £5.99
- [ ] Dame Edna Everage *John Lahr* £5.99
- [ ] Number *John McLeish* £5.99
- [ ] Tangier *Iain Finlayson* £5.99

You can buy Flamingo paperbacks at your local bookshop or newsagent. Or you can order them from Fontana Paperbacks, Cash Sales Department, Box 29, Douglas, Isle of Man. Please send a cheque, postal or money order (not currency) worth the purchase price plus 24p per book (maximum postage required is £3.00 for orders within the UK).

NAME (Block letters)_____

ADDRESS_____

_____

_____

While every effort is made to keep prices low, it is sometimes necessary to increase them at short notice. Fontana Paperbacks reserve the right to show new retail prices on covers which may differ from those previously advertised in the text or elsewhere.